ALSO BY KURT ABRAHAM

Psychological Types and the Seven Rays
(1983)

Threefold Method for Understanding the Seven Rays
and Other Essays in Esoteric Psychology
(1984)

Introduction to the Seven Rays
(1986)

The Seven Rays and Nations:
France and the United States Compared
(1987)

The Moon Veils Vulcan and the Sun Veils Neptune
(1989)

Balancing the Pairs of Opposites;
The Seven Rays and Education;
and Other Essays in Esoteric Psychology
(1993)

TECHNIQUES OF SOUL ALIGNMENT

TECHNIQUES OF SOUL ALIGNMENT

The Rays, the Subtle Bodies, and the Use of Keywords

KURT ABRAHAM

LAMPUS PRESS
19611 Antioch Road
White City, Oregon
97503

First published in 1997 by

Lampus Press
19611 Antioch Road
White City, Oregon 97503

ISBN 0-9609002-6-8

Library of Congress Catalog Card Number: 97-93651

First Edition
Printed in the United States of America

The future opens up with much that must be done.
Let not the doing intervene between the loving.

Discipleship in the New Age, v. 2, p. 703.

Verily, only the heart is able to penetrate
into all actions, all motives, into all entities,
manifesting discernment....
All the Higher Spheres are attained
by the tension of the heart.
This sacred vessel can reveal
all the creative exalted spheres.

Fiery World, v.3, para. 101.

ACKNOWLEDGMENTS

For permission to use copyright material, the author gratefully acknowledges the following:

The Lucis Trust (120 Wall Street, 24th Floor, New York, NY 10005) for permission to quote extensively from *Discipleship in the New Age*, by Alice Bailey.

The Agni Yoga Society (319 West 107th St, New York, NY 10025) for permission to quote from *Agni Yoga, Leaves of Morya's Garden, Infinity, Heart, The Fiery World, Brotherhood, Hierarchy*, and *Supermundane, the Inner Life*.

Contents

Esoteric Psychology and a Major
Technique of Soul Alignment

A Major Technique of Soul Alignment and the Purpose of this Book. Anyone even cursorily familiar with the writings of Alice Bailey has some idea of how extensive and comprehensive the field of esoteric psychology is. Esoteric psychology goes beyond, though includes, the physical-emotional-mental aspects of psychology familiar to various schools of orthodox psychology. It goes beyond the "persona" (the personality or lower self, the "mask" or "not-self") and explores the subtler, causal levels of consciousness. These subtler (and therefore "esoteric") levels of consciousness can be approached with what could be called a scientific attitude of mind, as well as a sensitive and more mystical approach, when we realize the special contribution of the *clarity* of the fifth ray of science. The *clarity* of observation, of thought, of identification is advantageous in the exploration of the relative abstractions of *quality* and *consciousness*, as well as in the more quantifiable realms. In fact, the two approaches---the clarity of science and the sensitivity of the true mystic--- are indispensable in the pursuit of spiritual knowledge, spiritual science, and esoteric psychology.

Abstruse as these studies may appear at first inquiry, after some careful investigation-application it becomes apparent that they are intensely practical. It has always been my effort and purpose to reveal something of the great practicality of the profound psychology of the esoteric teachings available to us. In this regard, I have come across what could be called a *major technique* used by D.K. in his work with his students and disciples (using that term "disciples" in its developmental rather than devotional sense).

The book *Discipleship in the New Age* consists of "Talks to Disciples by the Tibetan" and "Personal Instructions to Disciples." In the letters or personal instructions to the student-disciples we find a wealth of practical information regarding the application of esoteric psychology. The students are told, for example, what their rays are (which rays condition the soul, the personality, and the mental, emotional, physical bodies), what ray energies need to be developed for purposes of balance, what their quality contributions are to the important group work, and what particular problems of energy blockage or glamours they have that prevent full participation in that group work, to mention just a few factors. Throughout these letters there is a repeated and subtle emphasis on the *use of keywords*. This technique has to do with the *meditative and living application of keywords* that have been given to each of the students by the Tibetan, D.K., and that *constitute for them their quality names*. This is in keeping with the esoteric soul to soul technique of using the briefest of phrases, and, wherever possible, simply *one word.* This is in strong contradiction to the personality-intellectual technique of many words.

The purpose here then is to:

1. Identify what the keywords and quality names are for several of D.K.'s students.
2. Discuss the psychological significance and profundity of these quality names or keywords in terms of:

4

a. Their meaning on several levels.
b. Their relationship to the seven rays.
c. Their relationship to the various subtle bodies.
d. Their significance in terms of enhancing certain energies and balancing others.
e. Methods for building in the energies identified by the keywords, including meditations, reviews, written papers, seed thoughts, etc.
3) Explore methods whereby we ourselves can arrive at our own significant keywords and thereby understand more clearly the esoteric keynote and purpose of this particular lifetime.

The Keywords as Quality Names. In volume one of *Discipleship in the New Age* there are personal instructions given to 41 students or disciples. These people are identified with the initials F.C.D., J.W.K-P., L.F.U., B.S.W., etc. One would presume that anonymity was necessary, that initials were used instead of their names, and that the initials might themselves be coded in such a way as to conceal true identity. Interestingly, however, the initials do not refer to their names at all but to their keywords, or those qualities that present a most significant psychological theme for each individual person. This "coding" was never stated, of course, but it was only thinly disguised.

The overall and primary purpose of the use of keywords was to lead the various aspirants and disciples along their next step of evolutionary growth. Being developed individuals, their next step had much to do with unfolding and utilizing (or being utilized by) the specific energy of the soul ray. The words (keynotes) themselves at first glance appear simple, even platitudinous. But the meaning behind them and their effectiveness in terms of the psychology of the particular individual are profound. Not all the students were able to measure up to the offered opportunity and several of them dropped out. The record proves invaluable to us, however, as a means of appreciating something of the dynamics of esoteric psychology.

The question might be asked: How do you know or are you sure that the initials refer to qualities that were vital to the students' psychological growth? Consider the following paragraph that was given to L.F.U.:

> Your sphere of work is clear to you, and there you are both needed and useful, which is all that you desire. The keynote of your daily work should be *understanding,* just as the keynote of your work with yourself on all three planes should be *fearlessness,* with love coloring all your life. These are the three words which express what should be the color-tone of your life expression from now until the call comes for you to serve on the other side of the veil of life. Ponder on these three words---understanding, courage or fearlessness, and love---for the remainder of your life of service, for "as a man thinketh in his heart, so is he."
> *Discipleship in the New Age,* v.1, p. 227.

The initials L.F.U. evidently refer to the qualities of Love, Fearlessness, and Understanding.

To J.W.K.-P. the Tibetan wrote:

> Joy, wisdom and the Plan! These are for you the three points which must be matured. For

B.S.W. it was wisdom, strength, and beauty. For
you these other three.   You two are close---
closer than either of you have realized. Weakness
for you both lies in the failure of one or other of
the manifestations of power to flourish.   When
B.S.W. knows the true significance of beauty
and you of joy, release and fuller service will
be yours.
                    Discipleship, v.1, p. 158.

The initials J.W.K.-P. refer to Joy, Wisdom, and Knowledge
of the Plan.   B.S.W. refers to Beauty, Strength, and Wisdom.   The initials R.R.R. refer to Rest, Refinement, and
Radiance.   L.T.S.-K. refers to Lucidity, Truth, and Self-
Knowledge.   In many cases the initials and the keywords
find a clear correspondence.   In some cases it is not abso-
lutely clear as to what the initials stand for.
        In the above paragraph to L.F.U., the Tibetan made
the suggestion to "ponder on these three words...for the remainder of your life of service, for 'as a man thinketh, so is
he.'"   Only as we discover our own keywords and, indeed,
ponder on them, does the great value of this technique begin to reveal itself.   Before we discuss ways of arriving at
the keynote for our own lives, it is necessary to consider a
couple of cases in some depth.

The Keynote of Beauty

Beauty as a Means of Accessing Love and Intuiting the Plan. The first question to ask is: Why Beauty?
The keynote or keywords have to do with energies (qualitative energies) that are:

1. Part of the psychological equipment and need to be strengthened and brought forth more dynamically in service to others (often this has to do with the soul ray energy) or
2. The keywords refer to energies that are not present in the equipment but sorely need to be built in for purposes of balance.

We will come back to these two major points again and again within the specifics of the varied cases.

B.S.W. has the following ray equipment: (Refer to the appendix for a quick review of the seven ray quality-energies and some basic ray dynamics, if necessary.)

Soul.....................first ray of power or will.
Personality............seventh ray of organization or ceremonial magic.

8

mind.........fourth ray, harmony through
conflict.
emotion....sixth ray, idealism, devotion.
physical....seventh ray, organization.

At first glance there seems to be a good balance here between the 1-3-5-7 line of energies and the somewhat softer 2-4-6 line.

B.S.W. was a priest in the Catholic Church and probably held some significant rank in the Church. "To the militancy and devotion of the Master Jesus and to the vibration of His organism, the Church militant, you vibrate also with facility, for the priesthood had long been your chosen field of service." This is a rather "strong" description of the Church (for lack of a better word), but it seems to serve the purpose of identifying B.S.W.'s particular role in the Church. *Devotion* is clearly there (the sixth ray and the relationship to the sixth ray Master), and there is also a quality of *power* suggested by the word "militancy." B.S. W. had built a sort of "ivory tower---erected with care over six incarnations." "The first ray disciple loves himself, his power, and his isolation too much." B.S.W. is mentally as "hard as nails." He speaks "words of power and wisdom... with facility and truth from a storehouse of long experience." (*Discipleship,* v.1, pp. 624, 626. 629, 630, 631.)

The first ray of power and the sixth ray of devotion are strongly present in the Catholic Church, and they present many difficulties that have been obvious through the centuries. The primary need here, and one might add the extremely obvious need, is for the second ray of love wisdom, and particularly the love aspect of that ray.

To the understanding and the inclusive
love of the Christ aspect, as it expresses itself

9

in the 'fire of divine compassion,' you only respond in a secondary sense.   The awakening
of this compassion should be one of your ob-
jectives in meditation.

In you the head dominates, and you
sit on the summit of your tower,   whilst all
the time the call of the heart sounds throughout your being and in your ears. Yet you fear
to descend and walk among your fellowmen
in loving identification with them.

You must pour out the love of your
heart upon those who turn to you for light
and strength. Men today have need of love...
Why not begin preserving intact the principle of mind, thus permitting it free function
but using it with the wings of love and on
errands of compassion.
Discipleship, v.1,pp. 624, 626, 630-1.)

In assessing the psychological situation we see:
1. The assets, which are the strengths of the first ray, the
   order and organization of the seventh ray, the devotion
   to religious matters of the sixth ray, and the wisdom of
   long experience.
2. We see the problematical factors of certain ray energies
   carried too far or distorted in a personal way, and the
   lack of other ray energies.
3. And we see the necessity for exploring various means of
   correcting the imbalance. In this case the need is for the
   second ray of love-wisdom, and the means to that end
   include:
   a. A meditation was given to B.S.W. to help
      quicken the heart center and to augment the

quality of love. "Meditate upon the twelve-petalled lotus of the heart, visualizing it as a deep rose in color with a heart of gold...."

Discipleship, v.1, p. 621.

b. Written work was suggested: "I would like to set you the task of writing an article on the use of love as an interpreter of men. I commend to you the theme for meditation... Write with that understanding heart which is yours in full measure when you descend from your tower and give love both time and scope."   (p. 627.)

c. The use of the five day Full Moon period was suggested: "Pay close attention to your spiritual sensitivity at the time of the Full Moon."   (p. 632.)

d. The use of a spiritual diary "kept with care from the angle of the heart motive."   (p. 632.)

e. The use of the keyword *Beauty*.

Again the question, why Beauty? One answer has to do with the probability that he most likely has to access the second ray of love-wisdom via the fourth ray of harmony, the ray conditioning his mental body.

(When there is a lack of the second ray, it has to be accessed either through the fourth ray of beauty or the sixth ray of devotion.   When there is a lack of the first ray of power, it has to be accessed either through the third ray of intelligence or the seventh ray of organization.)

In the first letter written to B.S.W. it states that his field of service could be "enhanced through an increased beauty of the outflow of love and increased love of beauty."

11

If a person such as B.S.W.---a person who is strong, willful, in a powerful administrative position, oriented towards all questions of power and organization---reflected on the quality of beauty, beauty as it relates to love, what would be the result?

First of all, there would certainly be a softening of the "hard as nails" mentality. One would also become more interested in and attune more readily to factors associated with the heart (soul), and the related sentient-feeling factors. The feeling for things and the feeling for people would be lovingly considered rather than dismissed as unimportant little irritants.

Secondly, beauty has its own time out of time, so to speak. One has to make time for beauty because it defies scheduling. Beauty cannot be organized as one can organize a meal or a ceremony. An organized ceremony may or may not be beautiful. Beauty requires something additional.

Thirdly, the search for the elusive, additional factor directions the mind into the abstract and intuitive realms. The search for Beauty has to do with a *creative process*. Something "new" and something spiritual occurs when the alignment with Beauty is brought about.

In this regard, B.S.W is first of all advised to "avoid all static conditions. Many first ray people become static or crystallized, as it is the method whereby the first ray destroyers work..." (p.621)

Further clarification is given in a later letter. "The first ray person is conscious of ordered life, the majesty of ordered forces; the glory of the intelligent 'arrangement' of the powers which lie behind the manifested world in his rightful field of service. But to this must be added the power to intuit the Plan as it exists in the heart of love, for only love reveals the Plan and the part to be played in it by souls at any given time and place."   (p. 625)

Two things are of special note in the above paragraph. D.K. is recognizing and validating B.S.W.'s first
ray qualities, and, one might say, not only first ray qualities
but the one-seven ray combination---the *majesty* of ordered
forces, the *glory* of the intelligent *arrangement* of the powers.... The seventh ray brings a synthesis of spirit-matter
that lends "majesty" and "glory" through the "magic" of ceremony and organization.
        The second point relates to the factory of beauty---
beauty and love---as it or they enable one to develop the intuition and the buddhic vehicle. D.K. calls it the *power* to
intuit the Plan, once again linking it with the first ray soul
and adapting it to the specific psychological situation of the
person he is endeavoring to guide.

Making Notes on Beauty in a Spiritual Diary.
The Tibetan D.K. advised L.U.T. to give real thought and
vital attention to beauty and color and to make note of these
thoughts in a spiritual diary:

> *What things, attitudes, and words of beauty*
> *did I come across today?* Note these down and
> note also your reactions to them when recognized:
> a sunset of radiant color; a face or look which
> brought good remembrance; a paragraph in a book
> which illumined your mind.... Hunt every day for
> *beauty and record it....*
>   *What color or colors predominated in my life*
> *today?* Upon the physical plane---a blaze of sun-
> shine, the gray of a rainy day, the blue of the sky,
> the riot of color in the flowers in a garden or a shop?

13

Upon the astral plane---the rose of affection and of a friendly feeling, the blue of an inspiring contact, the gold of physical well being, the interplay of colors which your emotional nature can be trained to recognize?

What dramas came my way today, in my life or in the life of others? Seek for drama under the dull exterior of a person, in the world of daily happenings as you see it functioning around one. See it everywhere---the drama of life as lived by yourself, your environing associates, and also the nations of the world. Evoke and cultivate the sense of the immanent beauty of drama, and note the reaction of it in you diary; note also the lessons to be learned as you sense and study them.

This diary will reveal to you what you lack; it will train you in the objective and subjective recognitions which you so much need; it will lift you out of yourself and it will carry to you revelation and joy and an enlarging horizon. Ponder upon the words: Beauty, color, service, outer relationships, inner linkings."
*Discipleship in the New Age,*v.1, 482-3.

Although the rays of L.U.T. are different than those of B.S.W. the first ray of power (at the personality level in the case of L.U.T.) does seem to be the primary factor of concern. *"You need fuller emotional expression.* There is such an intense focusing within yourself as the result of a long spiritual struggle---with yourself and with circumstances---that pent up forces are gathered into the personality which must have release." The problem seems to be a combination of the first ray of power and the sixth ray of devotion. This relates the personality and the astral body; there is here a struggle for control, there is inhibition, or "pent up" emotion. The exercise with beauty is designed to "fill your life with vitality, expression, and make you radiant." It constitutes a "way of release." The great intensity of the one-six (power-devotion) ray combination (personality to astral body) needs to be off-set or balanced with a two-four (love-beauty) combination, which would bring a soul-mind interplay.   (pp. 481, 482)

The rays of L.U.T. are:

Soul....................2nd ray, love-wisdom.
Personality............1st ray, power.
    mind................4th ray, harmony, conflict, beauty
    astral...............6th ray, idealism, devotion.
    physical............3rd ray, intelligent activity.

In a certain sense, one could probably say that the problem is predominantly an emotional one, and that the solution begins with the emotions, that is to say, with the higher levels of the emotional plane, which have to do with right aspiration and with spiritual sensitivity---such as the sensitivity to beauty. Developing sensitivity to beauty, to color, to world drama is designed to lead one out of the intense preoccupation with the personal condition and with personal spiritual status. It provides a releasing attitude. For intensity (6th ray) of emotion, there is substituted the joy and play of color and drama (4th ray), all designed to link one to the love of the second ray soul, which relies on intuition.

The focusing on beauty, then, through the aid of the spiritual diary, becomes a real psychological technique for development of and alignment with the greater spiritual possibilities.

Are We Sure We Understand the Value of Beauty?
One of our purposes here is to consider these keywords in some depth and from the esoteric psychological perspective. According to Master M., the realization of beauty is rare: "One must know that amidst spirituality the realization of beauty is the rarest quality, and will be valued by the Lords above many things." *Leaves of Morya's Garden*, II, 117.

"More than once will you be asked where is the nursery of the beautiful garden of fiery energy. You will say, 'In the joy of beauty.' But learn how to embrace this joy of light. Learn how to rejoice at each leaf awakened to life. Learn how to respond within your centers to the call of joy. Learn to understand that such joy is not idleness but the harvest of the treasure. Learn to accumulate energy through joy, as by what else shall we tie the thread of the far-off worlds?" *Agni Yoga*, paragraph 546.

"Does an Arhat rest? You already know that a change of labor is rest, but the true repose of an Arhat is his thought about the Beautiful. Amidst various labors, thought about the Beautiful is the bridge and power and stream of benevolence. Let us weigh a thought of evil and a thought of good, and we shall prove to ourselves that the beautiful thought is more powerful. Let us organically analyze different thoughts, as we shall see that a beautiful thought is a treasure of health. In beautiful thinking an Arhat beholds the ladder of ascent. In this active thinking is the Arhat's repose. In what else can we find another source of benevolence? Thus can we remember when we are especially oppressed. When the shutters of selfhood are being fastened everywhere, when fires are extinguished in the darkness, is it not time to reflect about the Beautiful? We anticipate a miracle, we strive to break the lock, but the ladder of the Arhat is only in the Beautiful. Let us not sully, let us not belittle this path! Only thereby will we attract that which seems so miraculous. And the miracle, is it not the indissoluble bond with Hierarchy? In this bond lies all physics, and mechanics, and chemistry, and the panacea for all things. It seems possible with a little striving to move all obstacles, but the fulfillment of this condition is immeasurably difficult for people! Why have they clipped the wings of beauty?" *Fiery World* I, para. 177.

Detachment

Detachment---Everyone's Keyword.   Detachment, as a keyword, has been selected for special emphasis due primarily to two reasons:

1. This word appears as a keyword in the book *Discipleship in the New Age* with greater frequency than any other keyword.
2. Detachment is a crucial quality in the process of soul alignment and one that applies to everyone, regardless of ray type.

Initially, we can think of detachment as being the opposite of attachment, but we must be careful here, for, as with all keywords of this order, we are not dealing with a polarity, but with a transcendent third point, or middle path. (For a further clarification of this point see: *Balancing the Pairs of Opposites; the Seven Rays and Education; and Other Essays in Esoteric Psychology.*)

Attachment has to do with being bound to something, physically or psychologically, literally or figura--

tively. This "something" can be a person, a place, or a thing. It can be a sense of who we think we are or would like to be---the self-image. We can be overly attached to the expressed thoughts and opinions of others, to the point that we let those opinions control significant aspects of our lives. We can be overly attached to a belief system, to the point that we block out all new truths. We can be overly attached to a country or race, to the point that analysis is habitually distorted by the layered accumulations of our own historical perspective. It seems, in fact and clearly, that attachment is the norm, that the maturation process is going through a continued series of mini-detachments, and that supreme detachment is supremely rare.

One might ask the most basic question here and that is: Why detach?

Attachment leads to some kind of suffering when the attachment brings about a non-fluidic, non-growing, static state.

Attachment is related to form (tangible and subtle), whereas detachment is related to consciousness. Detachment has to do with a psychological vantage point that enables one to see, to observe, to be aware. Detachment implies being free or distanced from the form factor, and, therefore, being in a better position to make right judgment regarding the treatment and handling of the particular form factor. Detachment in this sense is not separation from form, for separation implies moving from distorted consciousness (attachment) to no consciousness (isolation, separation). Detachment implies *greater consciousness*.

Two Primary Levels on which Detachment Operates.
The detachment process can be viewed as operating primarily on two levels:

19

1. Attachment involves the emotional body, the desire impulse, and, therefore, the solar plexus center and the sixth ray. The two major centers lower than the solar plexus---the sacral center and the base of the spine center---are more instinctual in nature, involving the sex drive and the will-to-live or survival impulse. As the individual likes and dislikes of the emotional body and solar plexus energy are developed, attachments abound. Some come easily and are easily relinquished. Other attachments become central to one's life. One can become so identified with them that one mistakes them for life itself, even to the point of suicide. The development of the solar plexus center begins to distinguish human from animal. Excessive attachment is more of a human problem than an animal one.

2. The second level on which the need for detachment acutely arises involves the personality as a whole. In the first condition above we have an emotional focus that is corrected most often through a mental focus. Mental clarity can dissipate the emotional glamour. In the second condition we have an attachment that includes the totality of personality (physical-emotional-mental) and is rectified through soul focus (personality detachment).

Condition	Substitution
Emotional attachment	Mental focus
Solar plexus passion	Dispassion
Strong 6th ray likes-dislikes	5th ray observation
Personality centered	Impersonal
Ajna center, visualizing personal benefit-gain.	Ajna center, visualizing common good, asking nothing for self.

Personality ray....................Personality ray as sub-ray
of soul ray.

L.D.O. and F.C.D.   The following paragraph was included in a letter to L.D.O.

You have to cultivate more definitely than
you do the habit of mind, the trained attitude
of the Observer of life, of people and of yourself. You must develop the attentiveness of
the One who looks on at life and at the strug-
gles of others. It is necessary for you to learn
that when you can avoid identifying yourself
so closely with people,   refraining from suffering so consciously with them, you can be
of greater service to them and a finer friend
and helper. Therefore, for you, *detachment*
is an outstanding requirement and a quality to
be cultivated.   *Discipleship*, v.1, p. 130.

L.D.O.'s ray equipment is:
Soul........................2nd ray, love-wisdom.
Personality..............4th ray, harmony, conflict.
mind...................4th ray.
emotion...............2nd ray.
physical...............7th ray, organization.

Rays two and four predominate, accentuating the
special assets of these rays but presenting also certain problems of lack of wholeness.   The condition mentioned
above, that of identifying too closely with others, suffering
with others, is typical of the sensitive, developed, and caring
2-4-6 type. This sensitivity is right in its time and season, so

21

to speak, but, when developed, something additional is needed. Much of this sensitivity carries too much emotion along with it. It can be seen from one perspective as a virtue carried too far.

F.C.D.'s ray equipment is:

Soul.......................2nd ray, love-wisdom.
Personality...............4th ray, harmony thru conflict.
mind.......................1st ray, will or power.
emotion...................2nd ray.
physical..................7th ray, organization.

The advice to F.C.D. is to develop the "inner, divine detachment which sees life in its true perspective." The need is to be the "Onlooker who is in no way identified with aught that may happen on the physical and emotional planes, and whose mind is a limpid reflector of truth. This truth is intuitively perceived because there are no violent mental reactions or emotional states of response; the vehicles of perception are quiet and therefore there is nothing to offset correct attitudes." *Discipleship,* v.1, p. 146.

F.C.D. sorely needed detachment, due to the "vices of your second ray virtues. You suffer from attachment and from a too rapid identification with other people." It was suggested that he learn to live detached from personalities but to keep in mind that his relation "is with souls and not with temporary forms." (p.139.)

In summary, several points are made here that need to be clearly appreciated, as one endeavors to work with and build in this valuable quality.

1. The 2-4-6 types tend to be particularly susceptible to the problems of attachment.

2. Identifying with others, suffering with others is a virtue but can become a virtue carried too far.
3. The mental and emotional bodies, after developing into sensitive instruments of perception (the astral body is sensitive on the plane of sentience, and the mental body is sensitive to the world of intellect and the world of ideas), both need to become "limpid reflectors of truth." This facilitates the alignment with and integration and eventual fusion with the soul (causal body) and intuition (buddhic vehicle).
4. Emotional and personal relationship is replaced by soul to soul relationship.

This process of detachment, facilitated by the effort to *act as the Observer,* is also a *decentralization* process. The personality, once the center of activity developing *self-consciousness,* becomes peripheral to and the vehicle of the soul (*group consciousness*).

C.D.P. and Three Sixth Ray Vehicles.
The middle initial "D." most likely stands for Detachment. In this case we find another situation of imbalance along the 2-4-6 line of ray energies. Her ray equipment is:

Soul...............2nd ray, love-wisdom.
Personality......6th ray, idealism, devotion.
    mind..........5th ray, scientific knowledge.
    astral.........6th ray.
    physical......6th ray.

The sixth ray physical body is an exception to the general rule. The physical body is generally on either the third ray (activity) or the seventh ray (organization, rhythm). "Very few physical bodies are on the sixth ray."
(p. 520.)

23

"This constitutes a terrific combination of forces, but you assumed the responsibility of handling these forces in order to break the sixth ray hold which that type of energy has had on you for three lives in sequence." One way, evidently, that the soul works towards a developed balance of ray energies is through "overloading" the personality in one direction (a direction that the personality itself has chosen). This principle seems akin to the "like cures like" phenomenon of homeopathy. It is a method that definitely uses conflict and suffering as a catalyst for change and expansion.   (p. 524.)

The main question when considering the ray equipment of C.D.P. is how to balance or off-set the preponderance of sixth ray energy? Three points of emphasis come readily to mind:

1. There is the need to bring through the energy of the soul---the second ray of love-wisdom. The personality (6th) needs to be subordinated to the second ray soul. The second ray is a natural progression or up-toning for the sixth ray.

2. Since the fifth ray mind is the only access to the 1-3-5-7 line, the mental equipment must be carefully considered in terms of dominance and focus. In other words, with such a ray make-up, the personality-emotion dynamic would probably be the dominant feature in the life. What needs to come about to off-set the 6-6 force would be a soul-mind (2-5) interplay.

3. The third point to consider is can C.D.P. access any other ray energy along the 1-3-5-7 line? Are there astrological factors or environmental service opportunities that could draw out, say, the first ray of power or the seventh ray of organization?

24

One of the particulars of negative emotion in the case of C.D.P. has to do with *suspicion*. This resulted in "nervousness, forboding, worry, and that instant jumping to conclusions which are dire and full of disaster." D.K. referred to it as a poisonous weakness and "even when well-founded, it is still capable of poisoning the very roots of being, of distorting all attitudes to life and of bringing into activity the creative imagination as its potent servant. Suspicion ever lies, but lies with such apparent truth that it seems only correct and reasonable." Part of the solution to the problem has to do with "assuming more definitely the attitude of the Onlooker, who sees all people and happenings through the light of love and from the angle of the eternal values." *Discipleship*, v.1, pp. 504, 512-513.

Suspicion may not be one's own particular problem, and, therefore, may seem a simple problem with which to deal. Most, however, have something, or several things, from which it would take their utmost effort to detach. Much work would be needed before they could look through the light of love at some particular problem.

Another problem in this case has to do with the attachment of love---an apparent virtue. "You tie yourself to those you love and oft the clinging hands of love can hinder progress---not only your own but those we love.... I ask you not to cease from loving but I ask you to love as a soul and less as a personality." (pp. 516, 517.)

In a later letter, D.K. had to be even more specific, for the problem of the excessive sixth ray energy had continued to the person's sixtieth year. Earlier the problem had existed without C.D.P. being aware of it. Over the years, under D.K.'s tutelage and through her esoteric studies, she, evidently, had a good psychological understanding of some of the subtle energies involved. Yet major effort was still required in order to "set yourself free before the time of passing over into the clear cold light.... The glamour of ties and relationships has held you for years. The personality umbilical cord still links you to your children and it should have been severed (and rightly severed) several years ago. It would have been of real benefit both to you and to them.... I know whereof you are capable. You are not using the love of your second ray soul which can love and sever at the same time; which can convey the deepest love, subjectively and protectively, and yet---on the outer plane--- can set people free. Let me repeat again: You have no res-ponsibility to your children and never have had since they reached maturity and the right to live their own lives. You have earned the right to your own soul's freedom and ex-pression. Will you take it now and free yourself, or will you muddle through the remainder of this incarnation and, in another life, have to face the identical problem of family re-lationships and financial responsibility? As yet, you have solved nothing but you have made progress and your eyes *are* open." *Discipleship*, v.1, pp. 524-5.

We quote at length here because this is a situation requiring detachment, with which so many of us can iden-tify. It also helps to illustrate the difficulty of applying a single quality name, a single keynote, in one's life. Detach-ment is certainly most everyone's keyword and one that is not simply for beginners but for the very advanced as well.

Detachment for a First Ray-Fifth Ray Type.
D.L.R.'s ray equipment is:
> Soul......................1st ray, power, will.
> Personality.............5th ray, scientific knowledge.
> mind.................5th ray, science.
> astral................6th ray, idealism.

26

physical..............7th ray, organization,
ceremonial magic.

This person shows a preponderance of energy along
the 1-3-5-7 line. The first ray of power and the fifth ray of
science are the ray types to whom detachment comes most
readily.   Why then would detachment be a keyword for
D.L.R.?
The concern here is not with detachment from emotional attachments   His double fifth ray   facilitates a clear
mental focus. His astral body is developed and controlled.
"You are *mentally* magnetic, and through a controlled astral
body, you interfere not emotionally with that magnetic
influence."   There is no need here to labor at severing
excessive emotional attachments. The need must be for
detachment at the level of personality.

"You are learning the lesson of detachment with
rapidity, and you are gradually standing free from the clinging hands of others.   Just as the Great Renunciation of the
fourth initiation is made possible by the many lesser renun-
ciations of many lives, consciously undertaken, so the many
acts of spiritual detachment lead eventually to the severing
of the final thread which involves the death of all personality
attachments.   Then only those relationships are left which
are upon soul levels. Your task is to differentiate between
such spiritual detachments and those enforced detachments
which are undertaken on higher levels of astral awareness.
The problem of the disciple is to reach a point where he is
not hindered or held back by any human being and yet so to
handle himself as far as attitude is concerned that he hurts
no one in the process of withdrawal. The outer personality
claims of attachment are oft so powerful   that their clatter

and their rattle prevent awareness of the golden thread which links us with another soul. Likewise, over estimation of another person can act as a real hindrance. The chains must break, leaving only a golden thread between each soul---a golden thread which cannot break."
Discipleship, v. 1, pp. 311-312.

The above paragraph is of special benefit to us, because it helps to prevent a personality misinterpretation of the esoteric significance of the keyword Detachment. It does a person no harm if we detach from the "clatter" of their persona or mask. This requires skill in handling the drama of the self-centered and petty concerns. But most of all it requires that we are able to identify and subjectively relate to the soul within.

The keynotes, as we can readily see at this point, have to do with a technique that is *profound*, as it relates to the dynamic of soul, *simple*, as it simplifies and condenses many factors into a single word, and *practical*. The practicality of it reveals itself only as we work with the word on a daily and regular basis over months and years.

Seed Thoughts on Detachment.   The following brief quotes can serve as seed thoughts, or a seed thought can be extracted from them.   A seed thought is a thought that has profound meaning, but its meaning is only revealed after one takes the seed thought into one's daily meditation and endeavors to see it in the light of the soul.

The practice of detachment from self-concern
and self-conceit which the onlooking soul evinces
is no easy task.   *Discipleship*, v.1, p. 252.

The second ray disciple has to learn detachment while at the same time he remains "attached and inclusive" esoterically, and this must be consciously achieved and the attitude preserved.
Discipleship, v.1, p.575.

The first ray disciple has to remain detached and at the same time to learn attachment and to admit entry into his aura of the entire world in a series of attachments.   (p.575.)

Pain comes from form-attachment. It takes two forms: Attachment to the forms of earth, of men and place; attachment to the truth. They both bring pain and pain must cease. Ask the soul *how?*   (p. 405.)

This is not the detachment of self-protection or of self-immunization or of aloofness, but that soul detachment which works from soul levels and---seeing all life in the light which streams from the soul---regards everything from the standpoint of eternity.   (p. 130.)

Review on Detachment.   D.K. gave his students "reviews", These reviews are sometimes called daily reviews, sometimes evening reviews. They are on such subjects as Joy, Light, Detachment, Love, Karma, Indifference, Decentralization, etc. Sometimes the full text of the review is given in the book *Discipleship in the New Age* and sometimes it is mentioned that a review is being given, but the actual text is not included in the book. The reviews that are included in their entirety are: Review on

Light (v.1, pp. 198-9), Review on Joy (v.1, pp. 398-400), Review on Indifference (v. 1, pp. 430-432).

A review generally consists of some 15 to 30 questions. "I call it not an evening review as I care not when you do it, as long as you do it once within each twenty-four hours." The person is to take one or two of the questions in the review each day or evening and reflect deeply upon them. One goes through the questions several times over a six month or longer period. At the end of each month a paper is written on the subject.

Discipleship, v.1, p. 196.

We have developed the following Review on Detachment from passages quoted above and from related queson other reviews given by D.K. We have tried to stay as close to D.K.'s wording as we possibly could.

Review on Detachment

1. What constitutes a review on detachment? Am I confusing a review with a re-doing or can I assume the attitude of the detached Observer?

2. Am I capable of detaching myself emotionally from any event and thus more able to see mentally, with clarity, and without bias from the personal self?

3. If I use this review on detachment as it should be used, what will be the effect in my life and in the life of others with whom I am associated?

4. What were my emotional reactions to the events of the day? Did I fail to hear and see? Did I have feelings of fear or anger? Did I blame others? How can I prevent the above reactions?   From what do I need to be detached?

5. What were my motives behind the events of the day?

How did desire and self-interest come into play? How might I increase my horizon and my service capabilities through detachment?

6. Did I see and respond to true need today? If not, why not? From what do I need to be detached in order to respond to contact?

7. Can I detach myself from the clamour and clinging hands of the many unnecessary wants and still be aware of true need?

8. What causes fear or worry or nervousness? How should detachment function here?

9. Am I confusing detachment with isolation? Can I be detached, yet play my needed part and meet my responsibilities?

10. Was I detached from self-concern and self-conceit? Can I look at myself in a scientifically detached manner now?

11. When I am detached, can I merge myself with the consciousness of others and thus be able to think the liberating thoughts---the thoughts that will free my brother without interfering with him or her?

12. Am I confusing detachment with self-protection and aloofness? Does detachment lead me to the point where I can attach as a soul---serving, yet leaving others free?

13. Is detachment enabling me to love more abundantly?

14. Can I detach myself from my own ideas and my own truths, in order to see the right next step ahead for other?

15. What attachments prevent the full expression of the soul?

16. Can I view the problem of the day in the light of love? If not, why not? What attachments prevent

my full realization of the power of love?
17. Was I able to detach, stand back, and regard all things from the standpoint of eternity?
18. Has there been any pain today? Do I see the relationship between form attachment and pain?
19. How can I distinguish between detachment and the glamour of detachment?

The Dream As It Reveals Keywords

The Board Member, the Judgment, and the Pair of Short Arms.
The following dream was presented to me for interpretation:

There was a board meeting in progress. The meeting room itself was very formal. There were no windows. The chairs were made of hardwood, with straight, ornate backs. The table was long and relatively narrow. The walls were primarily covered with a dark red cloth drapery---the sort used as a curtain in the most prestigious theaters. I was in an adjacent room with another man. The board was reviewing both of us, and we were waiting, somewhat nervously, for the judgment.

The man sitting next to me was a minister. The board was presently reviewing him; my case was to be next. I chatted with the minister. He was a pleasant, likable person. He had obviously been working on himself, both to improve his character and to extend his sphere of service.

The board came to a decision. The meeting quietly broke up. Some of the board members strolled out into the adjacent room. There was very little talking. The minister and I moved into the meeting room.

The judgment of the board was communicated to us in muffled tones. Not much was said, but we knew what the judgment was. The minister, although making some effort, was not progressing in any significant degree. The minister thought he was progressing, but in the eyes of the board the changes were small and unimportant.

33

I was infuriated!

I looked around at the board members thinking, Who are these board members anyhow. Don't they know how hard this man has been working? Don't they know that real progress has been made? And don't they know that it is important that some recognition be forthcoming?

The board, in what seemed to me to be typical board fashion, replied to my outburst in a detached, cold, aloof manner, as if to say that my own emotional reaction was evidence of their correctness and my error.

I walked up to one of the board members. I looked directly at him, somewhat confrontatively, and thought: Who are these people, anyway, and who are you? I wanted to shake someone by the lapels. I knew I was jeopardizing my own standing, but my indignation was getting the best of me.

I grabbed one of the board members. He was a head taller than I. His face was puffy, almost grotesquely so. He had a second pair of short arms coming out from the front of his shoulders. The arms were about eight inches long. The board member remained cold and im-movable, as if withdrawing into a static power. I puzzled over the freakishness of the additional pair of miniature arms...and then I woke up.

This Kafkaesque dream can be divided into three points:

1. There is the issue of judgment, or whether or not to extend recognition.

2. There is the judgment itself, along with the reaction that it provoked.

34

3. There is the puzzling conclusion---
   the pair of miniture arms---that
   arrests thought and, therefore, is the
   catalyst for new awareness.

The judgment here is about the recognition of true advancement. The concern here is certainly about the *real* world of *real* advancement. That is to say, there is the outer world of social advancement, which may or may not be *real*, and then there is the true advancement as viewed from the inner side---which has basically to do, in this case, with character refinement and service expansion. On the inner side, nothing can be hidden and all matters are viewed for what they *are*, and are not distorted through veils of glamour and illusion.

When the judgment is perceived as a faulty one, then everything is brought into question, the main question being: Who are these board members anyhow?

The dream externalizes the inner psychological life, as do most dreams. The inner life of attitudes, feelings and concepts is externalized or outwardly portrayed in representative forms and events. This is done for the soul purpose of self-knowledge and group awareness. The personality is somewhat blind-sided or unaware of the effect that it is having on itself and in the world. The higher inner self or soul is instructing in a sense the outer personality as it, the soul, reveals the true condition of the personal and self-centered consciousness. It does this in much the same way that nature scatters forth countless seeds, with only a very few of them managing to germinate, sprout, and grow in those tough earthy conditions. But even when the meaningful dream is not correctly and clearly interpreted, some feeling of the content remains to have its effect.

35

All these figures in the dream then are part of the dreamer's own psychological condition. The main "person" clearly, to whom the dreamer needs to awaken, is the board member with the puffy face and the additional pair of miniature arms. The person is a "head taller", so there is some "height" or status. The "puffy face" and the "cold, aloof" manner indicate that a certain pride is distorting the view. The person, this aspect of the dreamer who is making judgments regarding the status of others, is not seeing clearly.

He is puffed up, perhaps in pride, and he is detached in the wrong way. The cold aloofness indicates separation and probably feelings of superiority.

The dreamer, to put it mildly, does not like the attitude of the board member. He sees a stereotypical attitude here common among many who have achieved some level of accomplishment or status. What he needs to recognize here, however, is that somehow this attitude has crept into his own consciousness. This is an externalization of an aspect of his own personality.

Another aspect of his personality is also there, and that is the aspect that *sits down with the other person.* This aspect automatically assumes the same level of the other person and can clearly *identify* with the struggle and the striving, the little successes and failures of others. There is no formality here that elevates and separates one from the other.

The puzzling or arresting conclusion of the pair of short arms indicates, it seems to me, a problem with *reaching out* and extending oneself to others. There has developed somewhat of a formal and somber distance between himself and others, and perhaps it is particularly on spiritually related issues. There is the need for this person to look at himself very closely and to take this matter up for an extended time very seriously. To facilitate this process a *key-*

word could be used. A new attitude needs to be substituted for the constrictions and limitations of the present attitude of spiritual blockage. The new attitude has to do with extending oneself in humility to others. It has to do with heart qualities of compassion and understanding and identification. Due to the power of the picture of the dream, however, the best keyword to work with might be *Reaching Out.*

The Dream of the Bridge, the Gate, the Smoky Satellite, and the Green Rolling Hills.
The following dream was given to me for interpretation:

I was driving down to Medford on the freeway with my nephew. We were coming to the first exit, but then up ahead I noticed a huge suspension bridge. I told the driver that maybe we should turn here. I didn't remember that bridge being there. But we decided that maybe we should go ahead; it was just newly built.

As we approached, there were men working there, spraying water on the road, so we went forward slowly. We got about twenty feet up onto the bridge when a huge gate came down. It was like a large fireplace grate. We stopped and the worker said, "You can't go on! There is danger ahead! Look to the left and you'll see the people of Medford." We looked and there was a huge log deck just off the bridge, tied with ropes. The people were chopping the ropes so that they would topple down onto the bridge.

We backed up and got out of the car. I was admiring the view of the hills and talking to the driver. The view to the left was of low, green, rolling hills. On the right there was a huge satellite dish, from which, as I was looking at it, dark smoke swirled and went towards the sky. The

37

dark smoke was all around the center of the dish.

The next thing I said was I know that this is a dream and I should tell Kurt. Then you were there in my dream and I repeated the dream to you. I sort of began to dream another dream, but I was awakened in the dream. Something in the dream said: "Wake up and write this down for Kurt." So I did.

The dream is divided into three parts
1. The approach to the bridge. Here we have the established pattern.
2. The problem at the bridge. The nature of the difficulty of the established pattern is somewhat revealed, forcing new decisions.
3. The presentation of the new possibilities. The new possibilities are not without their complications.

The way, at first, is an everyday familiar way, but then a bridge appears, which arrests the dreamer's attention, sparking the possibility of new awareness. A bridge generally symbolizes a bridge in consciousness or a transition over water (which on one level represents the emotional element) onto a relatively higher (subtler, more refined) level of consciousness with its accompanying "new" (to the individual) set of values and natural laws.

The first "fork in the road", so to speak, or point requiring decision, has to do with taking either the first exit or continuing on down the road. "Maybe we should turn, maybe we should go ahead." The particular or special point about the bridge at first has to do simply with the fact that *it is new*. The newness of the situation, one might say, pulls the dreamer on and up onto the bridge. This is an habitual, automatic reaction. Youth will often take the new direction-experience without much forethought.   Sometimes simple curiosity is the attracting factor.   In this case, we have a mature person whose Sun Sign is Aries. One of the characteristics of the Aries person has to do with the tendency to jump into new situations with enthusiasm and confidence, almost as a matter of routine.

On the bridge there is "water on the road", a grate-like gate, and people, somehow suspended on top of the bridge, trying to chop themselves free of their log deck structure.

The water (of the emotion) forces one here to "go slowly."   Some people in dreams swim fearlessly even in tidal waves. Not so in this case. The water-emotion factor is very small. That is to say, when a little appears, it appears as a danger, requiring one to slow down and move cautiously.   At this point it seems that we have more of a mind-physical (Air-Earth) focus and interplay, rather than a feeling-intuitive one.

The huge gate drops in front of them. The way is blocked. There is a seriousness to this. This is not a fork in the road. The person has no real choice here.   She simply cannot go on in the habitual pattern of crossing every new bridge that comes along.

The question then is, Why? And the answer is: Well, look what happened to the people of Medford. Basically, they have gotten themselves into a position that is too high.That is to say, a log deck is a rather solid structure that is generally elevated but a few feet above the ground. Here we have something that has presumably been floating in space or up in the air and now is caught in the structure of the bridge. The people are trying to abandon this huge

39

deck (solidly constructed but dangerously out of place), so that they can fall *down* upon the bridge.

The danger then is constructing something mentally, something that seems solid enough to be sure, but really isn't grounded at all. There is a need really to bring in the sentient-feeling factor and slow down. It may seem that there is a good plan, a good idea, and a mental-physical interplay---the kind that enables one to think clearly and to get things done. But sometimes the idea, the planning, loses its moorings, so to speak, and drifts off into an impractical venture. Nothing then works out according to plan. Indeed, one is forced to back-track, in order to determine just exactly where things went wrong. The feeling factor is the sensitive and seasoned factor that can help relate the idea to the craft of execution, one might say. The feeling factor can also tap into those realms higher than intellect.

So, what to do? First of all there is the nephew. The nephew is described as an "easy going, happy person." That quality then is there, as a part of her, but it is not in any significantly influential position. The nephew seems to be going along for the ride. He doesn't have any suggestions, doesn't take any action, makes no decisions. We could presume, tentatively, that this more easy going, happy quality is one that is present but needs to be empowered.

Secondly, there is a need to go back. Instead of proceeding, as a matter of routine, over every new bridge that comes along, there is a need to take the exit. to say no to all the new projects. We have here a person who takes duty and service very seriously. This person is actually quite over-extended in her selfless work for others. In going back, one is actually taking a lower road or one close to the grounding of the earth element, but this way is also not without its dangers.

On the lower road we have a "right" and "left" way. The "right" is the more conservative and, again, the habitual way. In this case, it is clearly not the way, and careful dif-ferentiation must be made here.

On the left are "low, green, rolling hills." On the right is a huge satellite dish, which is emitting dark smoke. A satellite dish is used to receive television transmissions. It is a symbol not of the Water or Earth elements but of Air. It suggests the grid of the brain or an aspect of the mind that receives thoughts and ideas. With the dark smoke we have a symbol of Fire, but it is a negative Fire. One has here then a negative Air-Fire condition, which suggests a misuse of the lower-mind or intellectual faculties. The mis-use of these faculties could follow one or several courses. If the wires are burning up, then there is an energy overload. There is too much intellectual activity of some sort or another. There is a lack of balance vis-à-vis the other elements and vehicles.

The solution is here, on the road that goes down and stays close to the Earth and the Water, and in the view that gazes out over the low green, rolling hills. The solution is not up in the Air and it is not in crossing new bridges at this time. But even here, looking out over the green, rolling hills, there is a tendency for the intellect to get engaged and to cloud the way with its dark smoke. So even where the solution is apparent, needed work must be done to prevent a certain habit of intellect from interfering.

The low green, rolling hills suggest several things. As already stated, there is a Water-Earth connection here. One is grounded. The feeling nature is consulted always. There is then a close integration of the emotional-physical realms. In attempting to be of service to others, one does not negate or ignore one's own feelings. One does not serve

41

to the point of erasing one's own real needs.

It should be noted that in other cases this whole matter could be reversed. In other words, there are people who are well grounded and well integrated in respect to the Earth-Water elements, but they lack intellectual development and fear crossing the bridge into new realms of thought and being. But for others who have nicely sped along with good thought but blocked emotion, or unduly controlled-inhibited emotion, they need to go back and attend to their own right emotional development.

The quality of Beauty is a major factor here, for it has much to do with the green, rolling hills. As discussed earlier, beauty has to do with a 2-4 (love-wisdom and beauty-harmony) ray combination. As it brings in love, we are applying a healing-soothing energy, and this is exactly what it needed here. There may very well be a particular healing quality of green applicable to this person.

The two keywords that can be extracted from the dream are Beauty and Rest. There is the need to rest from too much thinking, too much intellectualizing, rest from too many new projects, too much pushing forward, too much work, rest from assuming too many responsibilities at a given level. These two qualities will bring in a balance, leading to wholeness.

As one takes the keywords into one's daily meditation, many practical steps would occur to one that would facilitate and enhance the building in of the needed qualities. For example, in this case one could develop a visualization of the color green and of the rolling hills as they embody a soothing, healing, peaceful energy---an energy that stills the emotional body (solar plexus center) and radiates a loving-healing serenity (heart center) into all situations and relationships. Also, this person could simply spend more time in nature. For recuperative purposes, this person could relinquish some of the stressful work commitments and do such things as gardening, reading of the right book, listening to the right music, etc. We are looking at a person who has worked very hard, and who has given extensively of her time and energy for the sake of others.

The personality tends to follow a work-rest, work-play, work-indulgence, or an activity-inertia (rajas-tamas) interplay. At the "discipleship" level, or when the energy of the higher self or soul comes more dominantly into play, this pattern changes. One tends to "rest" in another type of work. One finds a situation, as in companion planting, where one type of work rejuvenates when placed beside another type of work. We also find then *rhythm* or satva replacing the activity-rest (rajas-tamas) interplay. In the competition between the tortoise and the hare, the tortoise wins the race. The slow but steady rhythm prevails over the burst of speed (often a disorganized, agitated activity) followed by inertia. There is no hurry, but there is no time to lose.

In this case, *rest* becomes a keyword, for the "gate has come down" and one must cease from overly strenuous activity. Yet, one rests in another type of activity---an activity that brings in the neglected feeling or sentient nature for purposes of rounding out the emotional equipment, for wholeness, and for alignment with the higher self or soul (via sentience as well as mind).

The keyword *restfulness* was given to one of D.K.'s students R.R.R., which we shall discuss later in the book.

43

Decentralization---Learning to Step Aside

Five Stages of Decentralization.   The notion of being *decentralized* may be somewhat puzzling to personality. A person who is developing "personality" in the technical sense of that term (which includes the coordination and integration of "good physical development, sound emotional control, and mental development" , see *Esoteric Psychology, v.1,* p.263-7) is necessarily "centralized." During subsequent stages, decentralization becomes increasingly necessary and has to do with a recognition of the illusion-producing-tendency of the personal perspective. It has to do with a "shift in center" from personality to soul---one of the distinctions being that the soul or higher Self *knows it is not the center.*

There is a most interesting, but brief, characterization of decentralization in the book *Esoteric Healing* (p.344):

1. The mystical extrovert.
2. The "one who steps aside from the center."
3. The "one who lives upon the periphery of the heart."
4. The "one who hovers over the central lotus."

5. The 'distant one who sees from far away, yet lives within the form of all that is."

These seem clearly to be unfolding, sequential stages in an on-going decentralization process. Also, D.K. is probably quoting here from what he calls *The Old Commentary*, which always designates the large picture.

The phrase " mystical extrovert" seems to be a contradiction. The mystic, generally, is one who withdraws from society in order to facilitate an inner communication with the divine. This quest is one of introversion, not extroversion. The term "mystical extrovert" suggests a period *after the vision*. Before the communication or vision, there is the self-centeredness of wanting a personal vision. This stage is often characterized by a high degree of unconscious selfishness. This attitude may actually delay the vision for many long years. *After* the vision-communication, the mystic *turns*, as it were, and seeks to externalize the vision via outer work and service. We find then some degree of extroversion and the beginning stages of decentralization.

The second stage, as noted, is the "one who steps aside from the center." Contrasting these first two stages, we find that during the first stage there tends to be a strong emotional content and focus, and during the second stage there tends to be a struggle to achieve more of a stabilized mental focus. The mystical extrovert finds him/herself in a very probationary stage---a stage of let's wait and see how the responsibility of the vision is handled. The vision, as it charges the emotional body, impels one to move outwardly. The surge of the vision pushes one in that direction. In the second stage, instead of a surge of feeling, there tends to be more of mental-analytical process. A choice, a decision, is made over and over again, and that choice has to do with "stepping aside from the center."

To clarify, it might help to look at this in terms of group dynamics. At a certain stage of spiritually oriented groups, one finds, it seems to me, a peculiar and difficult situation. In the early stages many people in such groups tend to be mystical extroverts. They have had some real spiritual experience and contact, and they seek in some way to externalize their profound insight and visionary experience. The true group process, however, hardly even begins to function, for they have not yet begun to "step aside." They are too taken up with their own vision or are too pre-occupied with their personal role in the work. Such spiritually oriented groups are often more difficult to work with than ordinary groups, for---like a religious war--- everyone feels that God is on their side (if I may exaggerate in order to make a point).

What does it mean "to step aside"? Does this mean that one steps aside and lets others rule and dominate, others who are in various stages of self-seeking and self-aggrandizement?

There is a paradox here. As one steps aside and relinquishes the personal point of view, one tends:
- to listen (not only to words but to the deep hidden world of other people's meaning)
- to begin to see the other
- to see how to empower others
- to serve others in a multitude of subtle and self-effacing ways
- to work more behind the scenes or invisibly
- to realize where the vision or direction can come through, knowing that the "vision" can come through anywhere, and certainly

not just through one's own little self.

One steps aside from one's gender, one's nationality, one's race. One steps aside, in a sense, almost from the vision itself, or from any *personal role* in the externalizing of the vision. Indeed, wherever possible, others can do the work just as well or probably better than oneself. Realizing this, one moves then into what could be called true group work, for one is very slowly becoming decentralized.

The third stage is the "one who lives upon the periphery of the heart." Once again we have a focus or *center that is not centralized.*

One way of interpreting this is to say that "to live on the periphery of the heart" is to live on the periphery of the Ashram. One has been tested. One has been found willing to *step aside.* One's work, then, moves imperceptibly into the outer peripheral fringes of the Group Work---the Work that has continuity and Purpose. The word "periphery" suggests primarily two factors: 1) activity, and 2) a subservient or secondary status.

To be on the periphery of the heart (or Ashram or soul) is to be involved in the *activity* of the Ashram. This is not the heart of the Ashram, neither is it the Central Life. Realizing that, one cannot be centralized. For the good of the whole, such activity can be psychically supported or not supported at any time. Work becomes important when there is no self-importance to interfere with the work.

The mystical extrovert is still aspirational, with emotional ups and downs. He is impelled outward from his self-centeredness.

The one who steps aside learns process and technique, detachment and observation. The mental choice to decentralize and observe anew.

The one on the periphery of the heart assumes some responsibility for some piece of work that is part of the Work. He becomes stabilized in decentralization. There is no such thing as "my" work or "my" group. There is no return, no recognition.

As we keep moving up the scale, we find the fourth stage of the "one who hovers over the central lotus." Again, we find what would appear to be at first a central point, but then our attention is called to another point, indicating decentralization.

The "lotus" is often used as a symbol of the soul. The "central lotus" could represent here the spiritual Hierarchy of the planet that stands as guide to evolving humanity. We are told that Christ stands at the head of Hierarchy. Here, one would tend to think, is truly One at the Center. Yet here too, if our interpretation is correct, we find a decentralized position. The "one who hovers above the central lotus" has similarities to the "one who stands aside." "Hovering above" implies one who nurtures, oversees, and guides, while at the same time relinquishing much control and granting much freedom. Hovering above is a detached position. It is not dictatorial. It is protecting and guiding. Yet it is not central. It is decentralized. Surely an occult paradox.

At the fifth level we have the "distant one who sees from afar, yet lives within the form of all that is." Does this not refer to God---distant, that is *transcendent*, yet living within the form of all that is, which is to say *imminent*? Is this not truly an amazing idea, to think that God---in some way we can hardly comprehend---is decentralized, and that this theme of decentralization is carried to the Most High, and that, therefore, *decentralization is an attribute of Deity?*

48

The Divine Art of Decentralization---Advice to a Teacher. The following words of wisdom were given to I.B.S.:

> In a life given to teaching (such as yours is) whether it is teaching physical plane matters or giving esoteric instruction, the teacher has ever to practice the divine art of decentralization. Being by force of circumstances placed at the center, the inner attitude cultivated must be that of a planned, peripheral attention, an identification with those to be instructed and loss of the constant sense of the little self. (*Discipleship in the New Age,v.1, 252.*)

D.K. goes on to say that 'the practicing of detachment from self-concern and self-conceit . . . is no easy task."

The habit of personality is clearly to be centralized, to perceive itself as the one at the center. Any group situation---friendship, family, work-business group, school-instruction situation, political work, church work, etc,---begins to offer opportunity to expand consciousness out of the self-centered attitude. The interplay between the sexes is one of the first situations that forces one out of the attitude of self-conceit, at least to some degree.

It is interesting to consider the example of teaching---both from the perspective of the teacher and the student. As students, the question is: Does the teacher know me. Does the teacher understand me. Is the teacher even interested in me? Does the teacher like me? Self-centered questions, to be sure, yet closer to what could be called the true center of the situation.

The situation is *learning*. It has to do not so much with the teacher's learning, although that is always on-going.

It has to do with the students' learning. Their learning is the true center; the teacher is *peripheral* to it. Good teachers *know* their students, and in knowing them, they are able to guide them in the unfolding-awakening process.

In order to achieve the valuable decentralized attitude, I.B.S. is given a few suggestions or hints. These hints are very brief and are in keeping with the Master's technique of using few words, and often *only one word*. A single word from the Master can provide a most meaningful direction to explore, and the exploration can take a lifetime. I.B.S. was given eight months to contemplate the contents of the above suggestions before receiving another invaluable communication. So much instruction at the personality level is quick, superficial, and expected to achieve instantaneous results. But that is certainly not the way of the soul. In fact, it is the antithesis of soul.

The goal here is the "divine art of decentralization." To achieve that, the suggestions are:

1. Cultivate a *planned*, peripheral attention.
2. Cultivate an *identification* with those to be instructed.
3. Lose constant self-concern and self-conceit.

I italicize two words here, because they seem to me to be of special importance. Without the *planning*, chances are that there will not be much progress made. It is often the planning--- the review of what has happened, the seeing of the situation in a new light, the re-thinking of the situation, the use of the imagination to develop new ways of being and responding---that enables one to change the old habits and patterns.

Also a keyword here is *identification*. This is the substitute activity. This is the attitude akin to soul that replaces personality self-centeredness. Clearly it takes much thought and work to identify with those who are different than we are: different in age, different in social environment, level of understanding, astrological type, ray type, gender, cultural heritage, etc. Understanding something of the astrological and ray influences, and point upon the Path, greatly facilitates identification.

After one *plans*, and one *identifies*, then the constant self-concern and self-conceit steadily diminish. Self-preoccupation is replaced by the soul-satisfying urge to serve.

A Review on Decentralization

Taking primarily statements from the Tibetan, we have
developed a short and useful daily review on
decentralization.

1. Have I primarily tried to extrovert "my" vision today, or
   have I been able to "step aside"?

2. Has stepping aside from self-preoccupation enabled me
   to see, observe, and understand others in a better way?
   Has this understanding led to greater service? Did I
   seize the opportunity to serve?

3. What are my reasons for wanting to be decentralized?
   Does the soul lie behind this urge?

4. If circumstances placed me today in the position of being
   the one at the center, was I able to bring my attention to
   the periphery and decentralize from the personal self?

5. From whence stems self-conceit and self-concern? Are
   these attitudes linking or separating? Are they based on
   truth or illusion?

6. If we stand "on the periphery of the heart", where is our
   focus of thought and what is our motive, our intent?

7. Have we felt any temper or irritability today? How did
   this relate to self-concern? From what did we need to be
   decentralized? Had I been decentralized, how would I
   have handled the situation?

8. My nature in truth is love. How can I manifest this while being decentralized? Through which body do I most easily express this love?

9. Have I been quick to defend myself? What would happen if I did not defend myself?

10. Was I proud in some subtle way today, or did I express true humility? Hoes humility relate to being on the periphery of the heart?

11. When people blame me, attack me, criticize me, or whip up resentment against me, how do I react? Whose problem is this, mine or theirs? Am I owning a problem that is not truly mine?

12. When people criticize me, is there some truth to the criticism? Is this an opportunity for me to learn something about myself? Am I able to admit a mistake? Am I able to step aside in such cases with poise and divine understanding?

13. Was I a "self-forgetting channel of light and love?" Or was I too much the center of my own picture?

14. In my speech, am I the theme of what I say, or am I forgetting myself in service to others?

15. Am I learning to substitute *the Plan* for my plans; *human need* for my need, and *the Work* for my task?

D.K. suggested on the review on detachment (*Discipleship in the New Age, v.1*, p. 432) that one "take each of these questions for two days at a time and give them concentrated thought each month for a year."

L.D.O. and His Nine Additional Keywords

Of the three keywords that were given to L.D.O., the only one that we can be certain of is Detachment (v.1,p.130). The "L" might stand for Love, which would help draw forth the second ray soul. The "O" might stand for Orientation, which has to do with bringing the soul energy through into practical and radiant manifestation on the physical-etheric plane. This latter quality relates to the seventh ray physical body and to the need to make right utilization of time, rhythm, and the Law of Cycles.

In the case of L.D.O. we see, evidently, a highly successful incarnation (in terms of soul alignment and service), and one that warranted, therefore, *additional keywords and meditative themes.* L.D.O. was given nine additional keywords---three series of three themes each:

Focus, Tension, Crisis, (Recognition)
Obligation, Service, Duty
Emotion, Intuition, Wisdom

L.D.O. had the following ray equipment:
Soul......................2nd ray of love-wisdom

```
Personality..............4th ray of harmony
                  through conflict
mind (mental body).......4th ray
emotion (astral body)....2nd ray
physical body..............7th ray, organi-
                  zation, ceremonial magic.
```

Orientation and the Right Use of the Time Factor.
The most striking factors that come to mind regarding the
above psychological ray equipment are the preponderance
of the fourth and second rays, and a corresponding defi-
ciency or energies along the one-three-five-seven line. The
only access to this latter line of energy is via the seventh ray
physical body.

In a certain sense one could say that *love* (as a fundamental soul and Christ-aspect energy) is everybody's keyword, and that *detachment* (as indicating a need to gain psychological distance from personal attachments and personal
identifications) is also everyone's keyword -at a certain developmental stage. *Orientation*, on the other hand, holds
special significance for this particular combination of ray
energies. It relates directly to the need to balance the preponderance of the two-four ray energy with something of
the one-seven line of energy, working through the physical-
etheric body.

D.K. discusses *orientation* in the following way:
> My questioning is based upon a tendency on
> your part towards vagueness and a lack of
> the sense of orientation in time. This is
> frequently the case with the pure mystic
> which you have been .... It is not easy for a
> person of your type to enter upon a course
> of self-discipline under the suggestion of

another, such as myself.
Discipleship in the New Age, v.1, p. 128.

You have to work consciously with the *time*
factor and you have to make out of life a
fuller expression of work well done.
(P. 130.)

You should aim at the outer expression of
the inner nature with greater frequency and
should seek to make the conscious link
between the outer and the inner
more dynamic and real. (P. 135.)

In the case of L.D.O. there is, evidently, a versatility
that is rich and profound. This is likely due in part to the in-
spirational link with the soul and the intuition which the
two-four ray energy provides. The "pure mystic", however,
can find difficulty in grounding, in manifesting, in making
practical and in adapting the flood of divine ideas on the
physical plane and in the human condition. Thus, the primary suggestion at this point is *orientation in time.* In such
a situation, we are concerned with direction (as opposed to
too many ill-defined, vague, and often changing directions.),
with grounding (as opposed to mystical dreaming or the
good-feeling centering of consciousness on the higher levels
of the astral plane), and with practical implementation on
the physical-etheric plane (as opposed to being the impractical visionary).
    The orientation in time must, of course, go forward
simultaneously with detachment and the need to be the objective, impersonal, detached Observer. One must be able

to *do* more, to *express* more of the inner high levels of awareness, but with less thought of self. The work itself, if it emanates from soul levels, takes one away from personality preoccupation.

Very often when a keyword was given, the personality would distort its meaning and would work on something that was actually detrimental to the original intent behind the keyword. The lower concrete mind or intellect has a way of *slaying the real.* The personality will often go to great lengths of self-deception, in order to avoid the real work of relinquishment and change. The Tibetan would then have to approach the same problematical situation from a different angle. Such is the case with L.D.O. Consider the following paragraph:

> The necessity to *do* and to *be* objectively active is a major glamour of yours, brother of mine. You need to learn the lesson that it is relatively of no importance what you do. That which is of major importance is to register consciously and all the time just exactly what you are doing. I would have you remember that right doing is the result of being. If your awareness of being is of a personality nature, so will be your activity. If your consciousness is focused in spiritual being, your spontaneous, creative and active service will be consequently by radiation.
>
> *Discipleship in the New Age, v.1,* p.135.

Earlier D.K. emphasized "outer expression" and the need for a "fuller expression of work well done." Evidently L.D.O.'s personality took hold of this suggestion and then *personality doing* got in the way of *soul manifesting through personality.*

Eventually, L.D.O. succeeded (in the soul sense), as indicated in the following excerpt: "I am pleased that you are following along the lines of your second ray energy, and are occupied with seventh ray activity; that means that, inspired by the sense of unity which is inherent in the soul, you are working on the physical plane (the point of expression for the seventh ray) and bringing spirit and matter together." (Vol.2,p.456.)

The key phrase is *orientation in time*. The quality or soul factor is *timeless* or outside of that limiting dimension. Personality functions in time and space. The meeting of these two requires a right orientation in time. The soul's purpose seeks externalization. How to express outwardly and through personality the inner truths of soul, without losing the soul's energy in the busy-ness of the activity?

In the above excerpt, we see that L.D.O. succeeded in bring these two factors into a balanced and right relationship:

Soul....................................Personality
energy..............................activity
second ray love...............seventh ray
                                        organization
spirit..............................matter
sense of unity.................physical plane
                                        expression

The power is in bringing these two together. It is very easy to be pulled into the emphasis on one and to neglect the other. The theme of the pairs opposites is constantly with us. L.D.O. succeeded in bringing these two together without succumbing to the usual pitfalls of working on the physical plane. It might be of value here to list some of the pitfalls to which well-meaning people often succumb.

59

Common Pitfalls in Organizational Work.
1. "Focusing all your efforts on organizational work" (v.2, p.443).

      This is a common pitfall and effects many who are suddenly swept into physical plane activity in service of an apparently good idea. The organizational work seems endless and most important, so this imbalanced state (focusing *all* your efforts) can come about very easily. For purposes of balance, D.K. emphasized the need to recall that one serves primarily through *inspiring* others and through *radiation.*

2. Failing to differentiate between a *living organism* and a *super organization.*

This is closely related to point 1 above and is really an extension of it. According to D.K., a super organization "is the last thing to be desired; a multiplicity of living organisms held together by cooperation, constant communication and possessing identity of goal and purpose is what the world needs today" (v.2, p.458). It can be noted that the seventh ray type is good at organization, but then also this type is susceptible to being glamorized by organizational work (just as the first ray type can be glamorized by power). The glamours here are many: the glamour of money, of activity, also power, the glamour of the business relationship, and, indeed, the glamour of building a super organization. Very intelligent and very powerful people can actually be operating within a thick cloud of glamour and illusion. The pitfalls for the aspirant here are many.

3. "Thinking your planned organization is unique" (v.2, p.447).

Obviously there would be a lack here of the basic spiritual keynotes of humility, detachment, and decentralization.

4. Failing to differentiate between the Plan and "my" plan.

This relates to point 3 above. Both relate to what might be called the *glamour of destiny*. In this regard it is very important to *scrutinize the motive* in order to determine just exactly what one is asking for the personal self. Can one work without the self-preoccupation? Can one lose the sense of personal self in the effort to serve others?

5. Failing, when the inspiration flows, to be properly discriminative and focused.

"You cannot possibly do everything that you see needs to be done; therefore, do that which will bring about the greatest amount of good to the greatest number of seeking souls." (*Discipleship in the New Age,v.2*, p. 448.)

L.D.O. was guided through these common pitfalls and, apparently, responded well to the hints and suggestions given. In the process he was given nine additional keynotes, as mentioned earlier. There is no need to go into all of them, but a few can be touched upon in way of definition.

Obligation, Service, and Duty. In the book *Esoteric Healing* we find an interesting series of definitions that relates directly to this theme. D.K. introduces this by saying that "the whole of life experience, from the sphere of nativity to the highest limits of spiritual possibility, are covered by four words, applicable at various stages of evolution. They are: Instinct, Duty, Dharma, Obligation; and understanding of the difference serves to bring illumination, and consequently, right action."

> 1. *The sphere of instinct.* An example that D.K. gives for this stage is "the instinctual care of a other for her offspring or the relation of male and female."
> 2. *The sphere of duty.* "The 'doing of one's duty,' for which one gets small praise and little appreciation, is the first step towards the unfoldment of that divine principle which we call the sense of responsibility, and which--- when unfolded--- indicates a steadily growing soul control. The fulfillment of duty, the sense of responsibility, and the desire to serve are three aspects of one and the same thing: discipleship in its embryonic stage...."
> 3. *The sphere of dharma.* This sphere of consciousness and activity has to do with the recognition of the part one plays in "the whole process of world events"----"one's inescapable share in world development." This has to do with "group work (as the Masters comprehend it)" and with doing one's just share of lifting the world karma, working out in cyclic dharma."
> 4. *The sphere of obligation.* The initiate, in working

with the Ashram, is "governed by the Plan; this Plan is recognized by him as expressing his major obligations to life." (*Esoteric Healing*, pp. 685, 686, 687.)

It can be noted here that in each of these stages or "spheres" there is a factor of will and a factor of encompassing a life or lives other than oneself. The will factor has to do with responsibility and self-sacrifice, and these directing forces lead one out of the limitations of egoism. In the first stage we have "instinct" seeking the well-being of another (a child or loved one), even to the point of putting one's own life at risk in order to shield, nurture, and protect.

In the second "duty" stage one may be "chained to the humdrum" in a self-sacrificing way, in order to benefit the immediate family. This is close to instinct, in that there need not be much actual thought involved. Emotions, however, come strongly into play. Duty here would include duty to one's "tribe" (club, company, union, personality group, sect, country, etc.). One may be called upon to give one's life for one's country. As a citizen of a country, one may have a duty to serve in the military.

During the "dharma" stage, self-sacrifice and the will are required as the personal life, personal benefit, and immediate return are secondary to the world need and the true group (soul) situation. At this level mind and soul come strongly into play. This has to do with the *soul's work* that aspirants struggle to find. Most people are involved with levels of duty. Few fulfill their dharma. "Find and fulfill your destiny" is the call that goes forth. Personal careers (in the personality sense) may have to be sacrificed (although duties are met), in order to be an instrument or vehicle for meaningful change and for the elucidation of the next step ahead, viewed from the group (soul) and world angle.

During the stage of "obligation", as it is defined here, the will factor becomes dominant. One could say that here there is an almost automatic response to the higher energies---somewhat like instinct---except here there is *full consciousness*. Obligation, really, in this sense, does not leave one with much of a choice. The Will indicates what must be done. It is not that the Plan should be recognized or that the Plan should be implemented. Rather it is the Plan *will be implemented*, because it is Life itself. *"Turning back to the Father's home, I save."* Paradoxically, one could say, at the initiate level, where obligation becomes a willing blending of the lesser will with the Higher Will, that one becomes for the first time *free*.

> *Instinct* nurtures and protect our young. It brings about the mating ritual.
> *Duty* enables the lesser or visible tribal group to move forward.
> *Dharma* responds to the soul, the invisible group, and the good of the whole.
> *Obligation* is to God. This relates to "Shamballa, where the emerging Purpose of Sanat-Kumara (of which the Plan is an interpretation in time and space) begins to have meaning and significance according to one's point in evolution and one's approach to the Way of the Higher Evolution."
> (*Esoteric Healing*, p. 687.)

Once again, the additional keywords given to L.D.O. include: Obligation, Service, and Duty. *Service*, as it indicates the impulse from the soul, relates to dharma. Sometimes the word "obligation" refers to obligations of the personality, which, in the above definitions, is synonymous with "duty." One of the main points regarding these key-notes has to do with a recognition of the *dual life of the disciple*. Two labors move forward simultaneously: responsibility to the family unit (one's duties or personality obligations) and the service of soul---the true group good. "Dual the moving forward...." The spiritual life is not separate from the world; the spiritual life transforms the world.

Focus, Tension, and Crisis. The keywords of Focus, Tension, and Crisis are, in a sense, an extension or further refinement of the keynote of Orientation, dealing, as they do, with the factor of Time and the Law of Cycles.

Focus is equated with inhalation. Inhalation is a gathering in of energies and can be thought of as a lifting of the focus of consciousness onto higher levels. Where is our focus of consciousness: on emotional, mental, personal, soul, or ashramic (group) levels? When is the rhythmic or cyclic time for the gathering in of energies---during a day, a month (the lunar cycle), the year (path of the Sun through the zodiac signs)? There is a distinction given here between "attention" and "focus." We can pay necessary *attention* to various outer details, while still being *focused* on higher levels of consciousness.

Tension relates to the higher interlude of the held breath and has to do with what D.K. calls the "initiation of causes." This is a moment of "exquisite sensitivity" and a moment of "alert conscious anticipatory direction." It has to do with the switching of identification into the "world of origins, of motives and causes." (*Discipleship in the New Age, v.2*, p. 449.)

65

The rhythm of this cyclic process extends then in exhalation, which is equivalent to *crisis*. "About such a crisis I can say little. It will take place in conformity with your ability to focus, in line with your attainment of the right tension, and the precipitation of the crisis will, therefore, give you release, freedom, clarity of vision and entrance into light." As the interlude of tension deals with the "initiation of causes", the exhalation of crisis deals with the "production of effects." (*Discipleship in the New Age, v.2, pp. 450, 452.*)

Following upon the third stage of exhalation (crisis), there is a fourth stage---the lower interlude of *recognition*. As the higher interlude is analogous to the held breath after inhalation, the lower interlude is analogous to the held breath after exhalation. This rhythmic and cyclic activity, as it is described here, has to do with the "breath of consciousness." There is an unconscious conformity to some of these cyclic rhythms through sleeping and waking, through the seasons, and through youth to old age. There are subtler energy rhythms and cycles that soul, the essence of consciousness, is aware of and personality is not (at least in any consciously cooperative way).

The high point of tension is one that has to be regularly, rhythmically, renewed in order that the outer work continues to be vitalized. It is easy for the soul-personality link to lose its vital interplay through personality focus and activity. Each personality has its own particular "style" for loosing the inner connection. Some we noted earlier in "pitfalls of organizational work." Also: "Without these interludes of abstraction, his work would slowly weaken as the tension, earlier initiated, weakened; his ability to attract and to hold others true to the vision would likewise slowly disappear, as his power to recognize became myopic."

Much care must be given, in order that the higher interludes are rhythmically approached. D.K. made the following suggestion to L.D.O. in this regard:

> Place one of the interludes at the time of the full moon each month, and the second interlude might come at the close of every three months work, at the time of the third new moon. You will have to work this out for yourself, but in doing so you could establish a basic rhythm in your life which you would never regret.
> *Discipleship in the New Age, v.2*, p.454.

In the hints regarding the "breath of consciousness", D.K. placed much emphasis on the interludes (tension and recognition). He referred to them as "epochs for storage" and the "seed of samadhi."

Emotion, Intuition, Wisdom. The third set of three keywords is Emotion, Intuition, and Wisdom. Since L.D.O. had a predominance of two-four ray energy (love-wisdom, harmony-beauty), it would be very important to distinguish between these three qualities. Initially, L.D.O. had a tendency "towards vagueness", which is typical of the "pure mystic type." One of the psychological problems in such a case has to do with a lack of mental clarity and a lack of grounding. One of the assets, however, in such a case has to do with the possibility of aligning with intuition and being able to develop true wisdom.

1. Emotion...feeling...sentience...the hunch...
   psychism...personal sensitivity.
2. Wisdom...quality of soul...experience plus
   love...meaning...sensitivity to whole.

3. Intuition...heart of the spiritual
triad...Oneness...synthesis.

Seed Thoughts on Knowledge, Wisdom, and Intuition.
We conclude this chapter with some quoted seed thoughts
for pondering:

"Knowledge deals with the ascertained and the
effectual on the physical plane and in the three worlds; wisdom deals with inherent capacities and possibilities of spiritual expression. Knowledge can be expressed in concepts
and precepts; wisdom is revealed through ideas against
which (very frequently) much mundane knowledge power-
fully militates. The concrete mind often inhibits, as you well
know, the free flow of ideas intuitionally impulsed; it is with
this free flow of the new ideas that the initiate is basically
concerned, because it is ideas, their right application and
interpretation, which determine the future of humanity and
of the planetary life." (*Discipleship in the New Age, v. 2,*
pp. 279-280.)

"The spirit, or monad, is primarily the expression of
will, with love and intelligence as secondary principles, and
the body nature, the personality, is paramountly distinguish-
ed by intelligence, but the soul has outstandingly the quality
of love which demonstrates as wisdom also when the intelligence of the body nature is fused with the love of the
soul." (*Treatise on White Magic,* p.40.)

"Intuition is a comprehensive grip of the principle of
universality, and when it is functioning there is, momentarily
at least, a complete loss of the sense of separateness."
(*Glamour: A World Problem,* p.3.)

"Intuition is the synthetic understanding which is the prerogative of the soul and it only becomes possible when the soul, on its own level, is reaching in two directions: towards the Monad, and towards the integrated and, perhaps (even if temporarily) coordinated and at-oned personality. It is the first indication of a deeply subjective unification which will find its consummation at the third initiation."   (*Glamour*, pp 2-3.)

"When the intuition is developed, both affection and the possession of a spirit of loving outgo will, necessarily, in their pure form, be demonstrated, but that which produces these is something much more deep and comprehensive. It is that synthetic inclusive grasp of the life and need of all beings.... It negates all that builds barriers, makes criticism, and produces separation. It sees no distinction, even when it appreciates *need,* and it produces in one who loves as a soul immediate identification with that which is loved."
(*Glamour*, pp. 4-5.)

The Dream of the Retreat House,
the Nun, and the Shared Living Space

The following dream was sent to me for interpretation. The dream opens with P.H. and her husband D. looking for a house to buy.

D. and I are in my car, driving around, looking for a house to buy. We drive up a hill and up a black driveway to a retreat house. It was for sale. We open the front door, which is not locked, and enter a beautiful old entrance way. It has large windows and high ceilings. The ceiling is painted white. The house is in surprisingly good condition. We look around. We think we are alone, but I look through the back window and see a woman running away. I go out the backdoor and start running after her. Sprint *is more like it.*

When I catch her, I realize it is Sister M.A., my old friend from Holy Redeemer. We hug and exchange pleasantries. I ask her about the property. She is there to guard the property. She tells us that they have to sell it because of debts.

I begin to discuss the possibility of the nuns keeping part of the house for conferences. Our family would keep the rest of it for living space. I've always been interested in

house sharing.
I awoke, feeling very happy, almost relaxed, about our future direction, as if God were watching over us.

A house in a dream often represents the personality. The house is what personality has built or what personality identifies with. The rooms and levels of the house, whether or not there are windows, doors, etc., tell us much about the present state of the personality with its sub-personalities.

The house in the dream is generally very positive. First of all, she is looking to move, looking for a "new" house. There is change in the air---a positive movement forward. The house itself is a sort of blending of the old and the new. We have the best of the old, as represented by the beauty of traditional craftsmanship. The old is not left to decay or left isolated and unappreciated, rather it is brought to the present in "surprisingly good condition." *There is something that has been cultivated and developed in the past that now has an opportunity to be utilized in a new way.* The large windows and high ceilings indicate such positive qualities as open-mindedness, having a broad view, expansiveness, and room for growth, particularly mental-spiritual growth.

The movement or direction in the dream is *upward*, driving "up a hill." This also indicates a slightly higher level of consciousness is on the verge of opening up. Something is about to be *integrated* here, which raises the level and increases the power.

Looking through the back window, the dreamer sees a nun running away. The *back* window and seeing an *old* friend both suggest something out of the past. What is the quality that is being suggested here? It seems to be a quality of humble spirituality, possibly devotion and good-

71

will, definitely kindness and service without drawing any attention to the personal self.

P.H., the dreamer, is in the power position. That is to say, she is the one who can either accept (include) or reject the quality represented by the nun. She could very easily let the nun go. The material demands and the spiritual deficiencies of the world are too much for the nuns. They are forced to sell, to depart. Yet, somewhat paradoxically, the nun both guards the house and flees from the house. She has to leave. After all, she is selling the house. Yet she hovers secretly in the shadows, watching over the house, the anchorage, the center for distribution of spiritual energies, hoping that it will be passed on to the right owners.

We arrive then at one of those archetypal crossroads in life---a point also where two strands of energy meet. On the one hand, there are the qualities represented by the nun---kindness, looking after the valuable traditional ways, spiritual aspiration, humility, self-effacement, devotion, etc. On the other hand, there is the person who in a position to buy the house. This latter more recent "strand" has been able to make her way in the modern world, with its materialistic emphasis, and has been able to provide for the family. Having attained a certain amount of financial success, the future may seem relatively secure. P.H., the center of conscious focus in the dream and of the personality, could simply let the nun disappear out the back door. After all, who would notice this quiet slipping away?

She sprints, however, after the nun.

The decision is quick, immediate, without reflection, almost instinctual. She did not know that the nun was there and she did not know that the nun could simply disappear. These are sub-conscious components. When this was brought to her consciousness, then the action was immediate: *Include the nun.*

How can the qualities represented by the nun be included? Here P.H. thinks creatively and tries to come up with some new ideas, ideas that are not necessarily the norm. There are primarily two factors here: One has to do with the principle of *sharing,* and the other has to do with the conference as it represents a *group contributing of knowledge.*

The main intent is to include the humble kindness and the spiritual aspirations of the nun. These are not "new" qualities for P.H. On the contrary, they have been developed in the past, but that have been neglected in the recent past and the present. These qualities need to be retrieved. P.H. is somewhat unconscious of the fact that these basic spiritual qualities are readily to unnoticeably slip away. One can lose the light that one has gained. The demands and the seduction of the material-form world can bring that about.

Possible keynotes here could be:
Include the Nun
Share Spiritual Knowledge
Humble Service, Kindness
Guard and Nurture the
      Spiritual Aspiration
Confer Daily with the Spiritual

From the above, one could easily develop a most helpful daily review of some ten to twenty questions.

2. Did I serve humbly without attracting any attention to myself?

3. Did I share my spiritual aspiration and knowledge with others? Was it appropriate? Did I miss an opportunity to do this?

4. What is it that I need to guard and nurture in terms of spiritual qualities within myself? Was I able to carring this sense of guarding the continuity of the spiritual through the day?

5. Just exactly what is it that I aspire to? Can I carry this with energy and in a single minded, focused way?

6. What part did beauty play in my life today? How can I increase the beauty of the day?

7. The past and the future meet in the present. Am I utilizing past spiritual knowledge and understanding? Do I have an appropriate vision of the future? Am I working towards the greatest good for the greatest number?

8. Can I confer daily, in the secret cave of my heart, with the soul and the spiritual realms? Do I see the benefit of this? Do I have the will to do this?

The Uncommon Keywords of R.R.R.

Restfulness. In the first letter to R.R.R. three keywords were given as part of six seed thoughts that were to be used in the six month meditation work. These keywords are: Restfulness, Refinement, and Radiance.

R.R.R.'s rays are:
Soul..................2nd ray, love-wisdom.
Personality.........1st ray, power, will.
   mind...............4th ray, harmony thru conflict.
   emotion..........6th ray, idealism, devotion.
   physical..........1st ray, power, strength, will.

R.R.R. has a problem with anger or an "occasional flare of temper." There is the related problem of "evoking too violent a response from others. This is due to the mis-handling of the force which flows through you. Get this matter adjusted and your present sphere of service will provide a fine training ground in the matter. Then your power to help will be greatly increased."
Discipleship in the New Age, v.1, p. 651.

The seed thought that was given to R.R.R. for the first month's meditation is:

Restfulness---The Place of Rest is on the
mountain top whereon I stand detached.
Flooded I am by the life and love of God.
That love I send to all my fellowmen.

In the same letter D.K. told R.R.R. that he needed "the sense and power of Rest."

From the personality perspective, we generally think of rest as that relatively motionless or relaxed state that occurs when we cease physical activity and also when we quiet the mind and quiet any intensity of feeling. Consciousness would be somewhat loosely centered in the easy drift of the astral-feeling state. It is generally a time of recuperation and may be a somewhat reflective period of assimilation.

What the Tibetan is indicating in the above seed thought is something that suggests a significantly higher level of consciousness than the astral drift. There is the need to rest the continuous nervous unrest of the whole personality and to center in the soul. This is, an indicated, very much related to detachment. Also, with a second ray soul the emphasis on *love* facilitates both the centering in the soul and the quieting, the resting, of an over-active concrete mind and an excitable emotional body.

The ray to be concerned about here is the fourth ray of harmony through conflict conditioning the lower mind. The often quoted passage describing this ray at the psychological level is: "Tamas induces love of ease and pleasure, a hatred of causing pain amounting to moral cowardice, indolence, procrastination, a desire to let things be, to rest, and to take no thought of the morrow. Rajas is fiery, im-

76

patient, ever urging to action. These contrasting forces in the nature make life one perpetual warfare and unrest for the fourth ray man."

Esoteric Psychology, v.1, p. 206.

In this regard it is interesting that R.R.R. at one point thought that he had a first ray mind, but D.K. pointed out to him that had he had a first ray mind, he would have dominated and controlled his astral body. (*D.N.A.,* v.1, p. 658.)

After the first letter to R.R.R. which gently introduced some of the difficulties needing resolution, a second letter was sent to R.R.R. that identifies the problem more explicitly.

You are struggling to be such a channel [of light and love], but you are so preoccupied with your struggle and are so aware that you are struggling that the reality for which you thus struggle is oft forgotten. It is lost to sight in the dramatic picture you have of yourself as a tortured disciple, with phenomenal difficulties in your life... Your physical liabilities are of no importance, because they have no real physical basis; they are related to the emotional nature, and are expressive of the inner storms in which you so constantly live. Once you have decided to de-centralize yourself and cease poisoning your body with the astral activity which sweeps you so constantly, your physical difficulties will gradually disappear. *D.N.A.,* v. 1, p. 654.

One year later D.K. again reminds R.R.R. about the need for restfulness:

Many of your difficulties are psychological and caused by an inner tension and
tautness which is really quite unnecessary.
To offset that, I would ask you to ponder
on one of the keywords I gave you when
you entered this group of disciples in
training---the word *restfulness*. Do not
work so hard, strenuously and furiously
at the spiritual life. It is a state of being and
not so much a state of achievement.... You
hear so much coming to you all the time
from the struggling personality. It speaks
to you so clamorously that the quiet and
gentle voice of the soul, bringing *radiance*
and *rest*, fails to make an impact upon your
life.   So rest, my brother, and cease this
violent struggle. Fall not into the snare of
many words.... But be as far as possible
a self-forgetting person, bringing joy and
inspiration to others and ignoring your reactions with divine indifference.
          D.N.A., v. 1, pp. 660, 661

     Looking at R.R.R.'s assets, we find that he is a
developed person with a good mind, a strong personality
and a wise soul.   He also has a gift for using words in
speech and writing, as well as having gifts of heart and
wisdom.   His fundamental sense of purpose is right and
sincere.   He is also in a position of responsibility, which
puts him in contact with significant people from all over the
world during a time (1937) of great world crisis.   So he is
in a *position* in which he can reach and influence a great
many powerful people, his sense of *purpose* aligns him with

soul and brings him to the esoteric work, and his *gifts* enable him to express the soul vibration through the personality. These are three important factors and not often are *all three present* in one individual.

There are problems of emotional storms, of self-pity, of being the dramatic one at the center and self-preoccupation. These personality traits are related to negative twists of the fourth ray and first ray. The solution is contained in the keywords Restfulness and Refinement and also in detachment, decentralization, self-forgetfulness, and divine indifference. ("Your problem is not to get rid of difficulties but simply to be indifferent as to whether they exist or not" [p. 659].)

Had R.R.R. been able to make the necessary personality adjustments through the right implementation of the keywords, he would have been able to enter more fully into the third word in the sequence---*Radiance*. This word, or quality, is most interesting and needs to be considered is some depth.

Radiance.   Dictionary definitions of radiance include: To emit something in all directions from a central point; to emit energy in the form of waves or particles, as in heat or light; to emit rays, sending out rays of light (or heat), to shine brightly.

If an aspirant or disciple is asked to ponder on the word "radiance", so that he or she becomes more radiant (sending out rays of light and love into the environment), one might well wonder if the message is simply a metaphoric one, or if there is in fact some esoteric scientific basis for the suggestion.

The sphere of radiation has to do with the "vibra-

79

tory effect of the centers" and constitutes the "so-called aura of the human being." D.K. also states that this sphere of radiation "is a potent instrument in service, and its extent and purity of contact should be cultivated by the pledged disciple."

Telepathy and the Etheric Vehicle, p. 173-4.

The sphere of radiation is easily determined by those who seek it out and who watch the effect of the radiation upon people in their community and environment. One highly emotional person, working through an over-developed and uncontrolled solar plexus center, can wreck a home or an institution.... One radiant, creative life, consciously using the heart or the throat centers, can carry inspiration to hundreds....

These centers are brought into activity by the cultivation of certain major virtues, and *not* by meditation or concentration upon the centers. They are brought automatically into the needed radiatory condition by right living, high thinking, and loving activity. These virtues may seem to you dull and uninteresting, but they are most effective in bringing the centers into the desired radiatory activity.

Telepathy, p. 175.

The aura of a human being is invisible to most of us, yet it can be "felt" or sensed to a degree in some way. The radiation of a human being is the aura, and it has to do with the activity of the chakras (etheric centers):

Major Centers .....related to............... Gland
(above diaphragm)
head or crown chakra.....................pineal gland
ajna center............................pituitary gland
throat center..........................thyroid gland
heart center..................................thymus

Major Centers....... related to........... Gland
(below diaphragm)
solar plexus................................pancreas
sacral center..................................gonads
base of spine (root chakra)............adrenals

A person who has an "uncontrolled solar plexus center," is a person who has excessive, often negative, emotion (such as anger, jealousy, hatred, envy, verbally abusive explosions, etc.). An uncontrolled solar plexus center can also do damage less overtly but, nevertheless, substantially through intense fear, disdain, malicious in-nuendos,etc. D.K. obviously mentions this extreme case, because even without clairvoyance we can still "see" it.

A person who is "loving" in a gushy sort of way, one who seems to be calling more attention to him/herself and to how splendidly they love rather than to the true need or to the true recipient, is also working primarily through the so-lar plexus center. A passionately professed or felt love is sometimes referred to as "falling in lust." The auric ema-nation then seems to be a combination of solar plexus and

81

sacral center activity---emotionalism and sex. As D.K. says above, "The sphere of radiation is easily determined by those who seek it out and who watch the effect of the radiation upon people in the community and environment."

The type of radiation we are concerned about here, radiation as a quality of soul, has to do with:
1. The centers above the diaphragm.
2. The cultivation of certain major virtues.
3. Right living, high thinking, loving activity.
4. Purity.

A helpful definition of radiation is mentioned in *A Treatise on Cosmic Fire*, (p.478): *"Radiation is transmutation in process of accomplishment.* Transmutation being the liberation of the essence in order that it may seek a new center, the process may be recognized as radioactivity technically understood and applied to all atomic bodies without exception." D.K. goes on to state that radiation "is the result on the inner positive nucleus of force or life reaching such a terrific rate of vibration, that it eventually scatters the electrons or negative points which compose its sphere of influence, and scatters them to such a distance that the Law of Repulse dominates. They are then no more attracted to their original center but seek another. The atomic sphere, if I might so express it, dissipates, the electrons come under the Law of Repulsion, and the central essence escapes and seeks a new sphere, occultly understood."

Our attention is drawn here to the fact that radiation is a *process of transmutation.*

When the essence escapes from the limitations of the particular form, there is a release of energy (radiation).

When the emotionalism and the self-centeredness of

the solar plexus center is transmuted to the heart chakra, there occurs then a radiant love, a blessing, and a recognition of the hidden soul within all forms.

The lower creativity of the sacral center is replaced by the higher creativity of the throat center.

The will-to-live of the adrenals (including the fight-or-flight response) and of the root chakra is replaced by the will-full participation in the Life of the Greater Life----or the Life in which we live and move and have our being. There occurs then the radiance of the crown chakra.

Radiation on Different Levels and in Various Kingdoms.

The "atomic bodies" mentioned in D.K.'s definition above refer to any bodies that have spheroidal, ring-pass-not forms with a nucleus of life at the center, including:

1. The physical atom.
2. A human being.
3. A "Heavenly Man" or a Being Who manifests through an entire planetary scheme.

The major point to be realized here, as we think of radiation as *a most significant factor in service and healing*, is that *radiation stimulates a similar activity (the work of transmutation) in other atoms, human beings, or Heavenly Men.*

There is evidence of radiation occurring in the various kingdoms in nature. "Radioactivity" is a type of radiation evidenced in the mineral kingdom; radium is given as an example. Interestingly, D.K. gives the eucalyptus tree as an example of "radioactivity," occulty understood, in the vegetable kingdom. He also states that there are "forms of animal life equally at an analogous stage" but gives no specific examples. Unlike the mineral and vegetable kingdoms

83

where whole groups can be classified as "radioactive," in the animal kingdom there may be "individuals" within groupings (dogs, cats, elephants, primates, etc.) that, due often in part to their association with people (the next higher kingdom), are becoming radiatory.

"The human unit (as it approaches 'liberation') demonstrates a similar phenomenon" (*Cosmic Fire*, p. 1061). In all these cases in the four kingdoms there is evidently a radiatory effect or energy release as the unit seeks the higher center and gradually transits into the next higher kingdom.

Radiation as it Relates to Motion (or Activity), Esoterically Considered.
The *Law of Radiation* is one of four laws that are related to a motion or activity known as "spiral-cyclic activity."

In order to understand the significance of radiation, it might be helpful to view it within the larger perspective of the three kinds of motion-activity. The nature of motion has been identified in the following way (*Cosmic Fire*, p. 1034):

1. Rotary activity.
2. Cyclic activity.
3. Spiral activity.

84

1. Rotary	....I Am	.........Internal activity	.....Brahma	.............Individual
Activity		of every atom	(Holy Spirit)	consciousness

2. Cyclic	....I am That	...Activity of	.........Vishnu	..........Unified group
Activity		all forms		consciousness

3. Spiral	....I am That	....Influence which	...Shiva	.......Unified conscious-
Activity	I am	impresses all		ness of all
		forms and which		groups
		emanates from a		
		greater center.		

Identifying motion or activity in this way has many psychological (consciousness) and philosophical overtones.

Rotary motion has to do with a body (an atom, an atomic body, a spheroidal ring-pass-not form, a planetary atom, etc.) rotating upon its own axis. The earth revolves upon its axis and, thus, "displays its own inherent energy." (*C.F.*, p. 1055.)

Cyclic motion has to do with the orbiting of the "atom" around a greater center of force. The earth travels around the sun.

The sun (the entire solar system) also has an orbital path around its cosmic center. The solar system also "revolves upon its axis but in a cycle so vast as to be beyond the powers of ordinary man to comprehend." (*C.F.*, pp. 1083-4.) This motion has been called *spiral activity*.

Interesting correspondences become apparent:

Rotary Motion	Cyclic Motion	Spiral Motion
Rotating on own axis.	Around greater center.	Direction through space

Personality..............................Soul.................................Monad
Fire by friction.....................Solar fire..........................Electric fire
Self-centered.................Group conscious....................God conscious
Rotary repetition.............Cyclic growth..................Spiral progression.

Rotary motion is "self-centered" activity---a rotation upon one's own axis. This motion has to do with the "fire latent in matter itself" and is the "prime characteristic and basic quality of the Primordial Ray of Active Intelligence." (*Cosmic Fire*, p. 141.)

One of the effects of rotary motion is *separation*. "The differentiation of matter is brought about by rotary motion, and is controlled by the Law of Economy." (*C.F.*, p.142.) Clearly, this would be the predominant note of the *involutionary arc*. (On the evolutionary arc, the Law of Attraction and the development of consciousness, rather than form, dominate.)

Initially, rotary motion is slow and characterized by *inertia*. Again, this is true of every "atom" or spheroidal form (from the "solar sphere down to the atom of matter that we call the cell in the body physical") during its early stages. The inner, latent fire is relatively quiescent.

Through interaction, friction, and relationship (Laws of Attraction and Repulsion), rotary motion increases. Inertia is overcome and activity-mobility occurs.

The rotating "atom" responds to and absorbs "extra-spheroidal emanations." Energy enters in from "above" and activates the latent fire, increasing heat (radiation) and rotary activity (momentum). The energy "from above" operates under different laws (the Law of Attraction and the Law of Synthesis). This type of motion is not rotary---*relatively* speaking, of course---rather it is cyclic (*growth* into the collective, orbiting around the greater center) and spiraling (*progressed* and directioned through space). This brings about or is accompanied by *radiation*.

Growth into the collective or cyclic rotation around the greater center brings about *awareness of form*, which is to say, *consciousness*. (Rotary motion, on the other hand, is total immersion in form, complete identification with form.) Cyclic motion implies *duality*.

The directioning through space of spiral or spiral-cyclic motion is the pull of or the will of Spirit. At one level this is understood as the will-to-live or the will-to-exist. At one stage-level, then, there is a will to hold the Spirit *in manifestation*, until experience-consciousness is developed. At another level there is a will *abstracting the essence* and bringing about a reabsorbing with the source.

"The first Logos is called the Destroyer, because He is abstraction, if viewed from below upwards. His work is the synthesis of Spirit with Spirit, their eventual abstraction from matter, and their unification with their cosmic source." (*Cosmic Fire*, pp. 148-9.)

Radiation as Transmutation---Transcending Normal Motion.

"Radiation is the outer effect produced by all forms in all kingdoms when their internal activity has reached such a stage of vibratory activity that the confining walls of the form no longer form a prison, but permit of the escape of the subjective essence."
(*Treatise on Cosmic Fire*, p. 1060.)

87

The forms referred to above are the "true forms" of the etheric or energy bodies. This brings us back to the definition quoted earlier from *Telepathy and the Etheric Vehicle,* which states that the sphere of radiation has to do with the vibratory effect of the etheric chakras or centers.

The vibratory rate (rotation) of the "atom" is initially relatively quiescent (inertia). It gradually picks up momentum (rajas) and eventually, through the spiral-cyclic influence (entering through the "north pole" or the depression at the top of the spheroidal form) reaches a "stage of such refinement" that the inner subjective essence (radiatory and radioactive) is able to "escape" or transfer its essence to "another absorbent planet." This life-essence "merges itself in the greater form of which the lesser is but a part." (*Cosmic Fire,* pp. 1062, 1063.)

This escape does not mean an actual leaving of the dense physical body. The escape means that the life-essence energy in the etheric body (body of prana) is no longer confined-imprisoned. It is released. It radiates.

The radiatory escape of this life-essence is not possible through self-centered rotary motion alone. It requires an "impulse emanating from without any particular atom, and therefore extraneous to it." (*C.F.,* p. 1031.)

This emanation, impulse, or pull is "upon the essential life by the essential life of a greater form; it is not due to the attractive power of the form aspect of the greater life." "The essential life of any atom, its highest positive aspect, is ever of the same nature as that of the greater life which is drawing it to itself." (*Cosmic Fire,* pp.1063-4, 1065.)

This seems then (to put it less in the language of form and more in terms of consciousness) a spirit to Spirit relationship, or a blending of the lesser will with the greater. It indicates the capacity to respond---via the higher chakras and the jewel in the center---to the greater spiral-progressive motion. The "attractive power" indicates the love-wisdom aspect. This alone is not sufficient. In *Rays and Initiation* we find the following related and most helpful passage:

> The great Ashram [of Sanat Kumara, the Hierarchy] is magnetic [attractive] in its effect, and through this magnetic potency (brought about by an inflow of first ray power) "units of life and devotion"---human beings---are brought into the Ashram as disciples in preparation for initiation. People are apt to regard magnetic potency as evidence of love; it is, in reality, evidence of the radiation of love when enhanced and strengthened by first ray energy. *It is the admixture* (if I may use such a peculiar term) *of love and will which produces radiation.* It is the conscious use by the Hierarchy of the power coming from Shamballa which results in the magnetic impact and the spiritual "pull" which draws the soul, incarnated in the body, towards the Ashram.
> *The Rays and the Initiations*, pp. 374-5.

The above gives us much food for thought. Below are some excerpts that can be used as seed thoughts for meditation, facilitating soul alignment and world service.

Seed Thoughts on Radiation. When we read something (other than simple informational facts), we generally recognize its validity straight away only if we already know it, if it is already part of the fabric of our experience-consciousness. As we meditate on seed thoughts, we are trying to access something that has not yet been pulled through into brain awareness. The *intent* or *motive* in meditation is paramount. The selfish (rotary?) motive is a dangerous one, and therefore we are repeatedly asked to scrutinize the motive, and to ask nothing for the separated self.

"The radiation of the Hierarchy... is implemented by the magnetic aspect. This is 'a point of focused fire, found in the center of the jewel. It stirs to life the quality of love which permeates the Ashram of the Lord. Radiation then can penetrate to the other centers and to other lives, and thus the Lord is served.' It is this point of focused dynamic will at the very heart of the Hierarchy which in reality implements the Plan."

The Rays and the Initiations, pp. 375-6.

"The process of transmutation is dual and necessitates a preliminary stage of application of external factors, a fanning and care and development of the inner positive nucleus, a period of incubation or of systemic feeding of the inner flame, and an increase in voltage. There is next a secondary stage wherein the external factors do not count so much, and wherein the inner center of energy in the atom may be left to do its own work."

Cosmic Fire, p. 479.

"It is interesting to note that during this round, owing to planetary decision, the process of producing human radiation or 'release' is being artificially stimulated through the method which we call initiation, and the short cut to intensive purification and stimulation is open to all who are willing to pass through the divine alchemical fire."

Cosmic Fire, pp. 1075-6.

"The healer must achieve magnetic purity...
attain dispelling radiance. This involves great person
discipline in the daily life and the *habit* of pure living.
inevitably and automatically results in radiance."
Esoteric Healing, p. 526.

"Another period of radioactivity occurred during the
time of the Buddha and many achieved Arhatship in those
days. That period was the highest point of what is occultly
termed a 'cycle of the third degree,' and a similar degree of
radiatory activity has not been reached since that time.
Human radiation of a very slight nature was felt about the
time of Christ, but it only lasted for a couple of hundred
years, and though individuals here and there have since
achieved the goal, yet no large numbers have passed suc-
cessfully through the fires of transmutation, and thus trans-
cended the fourth kingdom. The cycle is again on an upward turn; about the fourteenth century the human kingdom began to be noticeably radioactive, and we are on the
way to the fulfillment of a 'cycle of the second order' or of a
period of transcendence of a still greater activity than in the
time of the Buddha."
Cosmic Fire, p. 1079.

**A Concluding Word on R.R.R. and the Keynote of
Radiation.** In the final letter to R.R.R. (May, 1939) it is
indicated that he still had not gotten the emotional upsets
under control. He was still working on Restfulness and
Refinement, also decentralization and divine indifference.
"Unless you can learn to decentralize yourself, and cease
this constant self-thought and self-commiseration under all
circumstances, and stop visualizing yourself at all times as in
the center...and learn to see yourself as you truly are, you

91

can and do hinder the work and imperil the future construc-
tive work of the group" (p. 661). D.K. does not mince
words, though he always speaks out of love.

Some deep reflection on *radiance* might have helped
R.R.R. greatly to see the importance of the auric emanation
and the damage that the solar plexus "charge" can do. This
is no easy task for anyone to bring under control, particularly when the responsibilities weigh heavily. Yet a most
significant opportunity was presented to him.

We have gone into some depth on the word
"radiance" in order to show something of the depth of these
keynotes. They have *cosmic* overtones.

"When there is cooperation with the cosmic forces,
the sensitive receptivity affords union with the manifestations of Cosmos. The Spatial Fire can impart creative tensity
to the spirit which affirms its concordances. Therefore,
since the spirit of an Agni Yogi senses all cosmic perturba-
tions the link with the Cosmos reveals to him all paths to
knowledge. Thus, all cosmic forces resound upon the solar
plexus. The subtlety determines the quality of each recep-
tion. The whole of evolution is built upon this law."
Infinity, v.2, paragraph 347.

D.H.B.----Detachment, Humility, and Being, and the Twelve Qualities of the Heart

In the first letter to D.H.B. the keynotes were indicated along with the suggestion to build them "into the fabric of your life with the strictest attention."

One of the first lessons every chela has to learn is the growth of that inner detachment which will enable him to merge himself in the consciousness of his brother and so know and ascertain the best way to help him and to stimulate him to renewed *self-effort*. He needs also to cultivate that true humility which will force him to give all he has in selfless service, and then to forget that he has thus given of himself. He must have no thought of himself as a factor in the case. Only when detachment and humility are present can a disciple really serve. Cultivate, therefore, these qualities and continue the giving of yourself in service.

These are two of the keynotes which are specially yours, and these qualities should be built into the fabric of your life with the strictest attention. Your third keynote is *being*. Learn to stand in spiritual being, remembering ever that to *be* is a greater realization than to know or to act. The con-

stant effort to dwell in the Secret Place of your own soul and from thence to go forth into the world of men, pouring forth love and understanding, should be your prime endeavor.
Discipleship in the New Age, v. 1, pp. 416-7.

D.H.B. clearly stands for Detachment, Humility, and Being.

Humility of Heart or Humility of Head. In a letter dated March, 1937, D.K. made the following suggestion to D.H.B. "*Humble love* is for you the goal this year together with the expression of a loving, understanding heart, thus aiding all you meet. *Have no other aim.* The practice of this will balance and round out your undoubted head development" (my italics, *D.N.A.,* v. 1, p. 425).

In a later letter D.K. emphasized the same quality but with additional differentiation. A disciple reaches a point at which detachment from past achievements is necessary. "This detachment, based on a phase of spiritual dissatisfaction, engenders also humility of heart---a quality you much need to cultivate. Humility of head is largely theoretical and imposed; humility of heart is practical and inherently spontaneous. I would have you ponder on these distinctions for you will learn much thereby" (pp. 657-8).

D.H.B. rays are:
Soul.................2nd ray, love-wisdom
Personality........6th ray, idealism, devotion
mind.............1st ray, power, will
astral............1st ray
physical........7th ray, organization, cere-
                     monial magic.

94

The first ray of will can bring about glamours of power (when this ray energy is distorted by personality), such as pride of status, pride of accomplishment, pride of position. This would significantly affect one's relationships. Instead of humility, one would find subtleties of superiority---having attitudes about knowing more, being better, being in a position of authority, being able to judge others, being more powerful, etc,---all very subtle, of course, and disguised behind a myriad of social graces. Other people, however, can generally read such attitudes loud and clear.

With a first ray mind, along with a first ray astral body, D.H.B. would tend to *think power*. Humility would certainly not be a path of least resistance. When a person plays the power game at the personality level, the last thing they would think about would be humility. And if they did, often it would be a false humility---a superiority that masks itself as humility, an outward play of humility but an inward thinking that one is truly superior.

These attitudes of superiority are filled with glamour because, for one reason, they are unreal---not based on true spiritual fact.

The solution here becomes clear: The first ray of power needs to be balanced with the second ray of love-wisdom. Fortunately, it is the soul ray. The wisdom aspect of this ray has been developed more than the love aspect, in the case of D.H.B. The solution then is to build in the qualitative energy of a *humble, loving, understanding heart.*

"*True humility is based on fact, on vision and on time pressures.* Here I give you a hint and would ask you to think deeply on these three foundations of a major personality attitude which must be held and demonstrated before each initiation. I would remind you that there must

95

always be humility in the presence of the vision."
Discipleship in the New Age, v.1, p. 96.

Twelve Qualities of the Heart. The work of developing
the qualities of love and understanding, of patience and
humility---qualities of the heart---was of major significance
in the life of D.H.B. His first mind and astral body, and his
sixth ray personality, kept getting in the way of his soul
development. The first ray-sixth ray combination brought in
such problematical factors as: "judging with harshness,"
"surety of opinion," being somewhat of a "fanatical
devotee," being "hard and unyielding."

D.H.B. was, among other things, a teacher of
esotericism. The second ray is the teaching ray. But here,
too, the 1-6 ray combination got him into difficulty. There
was a tendency for him to fanatically identify with his own
way of approach. He expected other to go his way. He
was "wedded to his own methods and anxious to impose
them upon others. He is convinced that the techniques he
employs are the best for all. All disciples have to learn to
recognize the many ways, the many methods and the widely
differently developed techniques. Their attitude (when they
have learned this lesson) is ever the fostering, the interpreting and the strengthening of the ways and methods
which suit those with whom they are associated and
working, or those they are endeavoring to help" (v.2, p.
659).

Once again, second ray attitudes associated with a
loving heart would provide the way forward in this case.
To facilitate this, D.K. gave him a meditation which
included *twelve seed thoughts on the heart qualities.*
D.H.B. was to take one of these "twelve virtues" each
month for a year. (Actually, only eleven were given in the

96

book.) These qualities are of great value when taken up in one's meditative work over that period of time.

1. Group love, embracing individuals.
2, Humility, signifying your personality attitude.
3. Service, indicating your soul's preoccupation.
4. Patience, signifying the embryonic immortality.
5. Life, or expressed activity which is the manifestation of love because it is essential dualism.
6. Tolerance, which is the first expression of buddhic understanding.
7. Identification with others, which is embryonic fusion, carried eventually to synthesis when the head center is developed.
8. Compassion, which is essentially the right use of the pairs of opposites.
9. Sympathy, which is the consequence of knowledge and of the unfoldment of the knowledge petals. Such energy then is in touch with the heart center.
10. Wisdom, which is the fruit of love and indicates the awakening of the love petals of the egoic lotus.
11. Sacrifice, which is the giving of the heart's blood of life for others.

Discipleship in the New Age, v. 2, pp, 660-1.

Once again, D.K. indicates and emphasizes that there is a need to penetrate to the deeper meaning of these words and phrases. "Seek ever the inner significance and not just the assembling of thought upon these qualities. Most of the thoughts and ideas which will come to you in this connection will be well known and so purely exoteric.

There are, however, secondary meanings which are of real significance to the disciple, though almost unknown to the average man. Endeavor to find these " (v.2, p.661).

Identification---Embryonic Fusion. "Identification with others, which is embryonic fusion, carried eventually to synthesis, when the head center is developed."

There are two stages stated and a third implied:
1. Embryonic fusion, identification.
2. Fusion, or unity, seeing with.
3. Synthesis, or oneness, complete identification, being one with.

The effort and the question here is how to identify with soul, and, from what we already know, this may very well require detachment from the three levels of personality. It does not make much difference, for example, whether we, as personalities of intellect, agree or disagree with, say, the political or religious ideas germinating in another. The effort is to identify with something deeper than the often rapidly changing and developmentally limited ideas of another.

If we can achieve that identification with soul, then at least momentarily there is that sense of seeing *with* the person, entering into "the heart" of the person, and "looking outward" with the person, instead of the other way around. Generally we look through the veil of our own personalities *at* the person, and we generally fail to see anything but our own projections, which carry us swiftly to false conclusions. The magic ingredient or the particular psychological "chemistry" that enables one to see something as it *is in essence* (rather than as it appears to be or as we think it is) is love, a quality of heart.

98

One could say that there is a tendency for men to identify with men, women with women, and races with their own race. There is a tendency for management to identify with management, labor with labor, peers with peers, Catholics with Catholics, Buddhists with Buddhists, etc. All this is, of course, projection, because it is identification with self. When one sees *the qualities* that can manifest through an *endless diversity of outer forms*, then racial, class, age, religious, political, national, occupational, and individual lines *can easily be crossed.*

The heart quality of identification is a transcendent third quality (one that leads between the pairs of opposites), which is true of all the heart qualities and keynotes. In other words it is not so much a matter of too little or too much identification as much as it is a matter of *right* identification. The following passages help to clarify this.

You have necessarily at this stage the vices of your second ray virtues. You suffer from attachment and from a too rapid identification with other people. (Written to F.C.D., rays II, 4, 1-2-7, v. 1. p. 139.)

Disciples are apt often to think that the injunction to identify themselves with other people must involve complete identification with all their experiences, moods, reactions. It does not. It should not. It involves identification (through intuition) with underlying soul purpose and a consequent ability to interpret and explain the present. (Also for F.C.D., V.2, P. 463.)

It is necessary for you to learn that when you can avoid identifying yourself so closely with people, refraining from suffering so consciously with them, you can be of greater service to them, and a finer friend and helper. (Written to L.D.O., rays: II, 4, 4-2-7, v. 1, p. 130.)

From the above we could make a few probable suppositions:
1. One of the virtues of the second ray type is being able to identify with others.
2. This virtue must be carefully observed, so that it does not go too far.
3. Identification and right detachment must proceed together.
4. Personality identification---identifying with others' thoughts, feelings, and physical situation---is most likely a very necessary developmental stage in personality growth. For aspirants and disciples, however, personality identification needs to be relinquished.
5. Personality identification impairs true service.
6. Endeavoring to identify the soul of another tends to draw upon the intuition and helps to develop the buddhic vehicle.

We find quite different advice given in the following case: P.G.C. (rays II, 7, 5-6-7) was suffering from the "glamour of detachment."
For you, the word which brings light is *identification*.... By means of that identification the soul becomes at-one with all that breathes.... You...

100

need...a closer identification with humanity and release from a glamorous pre-occupation with what
goes on in the higher levels of consciousness and a
closer interest in the reactions upon the plane of
personality expression. (Vol. 1, p. 354.)

In the above case of P.G.C. we see a scientific fifth
ray (conditioning the mind) detachment that is carried to a
psychologically unhealthy (unwhole) degree of separation.
Here the second ray soul could help much to off-set the
separative tendency of mind---off-set the glamour of
detachment through *right* identification.
    From the above we can see once again that any true
spiritual direction, given as a suggestion, can be rather easily
distorted (by personality or the self-centered and selfish
ego) either in a separative, cold, distancing manner, or in an
excessively warm, too personal, too emotionally effusive a
manner. This must be one of the reasons why D.K.'s suggestions paradoxically posed opposites, in order to facilitate
the recognition of a middle path and a transcendent third---
such as *divine indifference, personally impersonal,
divine ignoring, attached detachment,* etc.

Patience---Embryonic Immortality. "Patience, signifying
the embryonic immortality and persistence which is a soul
characteristic."
    Patience, as a *heart* quality, is the opposite of im-
patience, which seems to find most of its agitated activity
in the solar plexus center.
    As with all the keywords, it is most interesting to
carry the word with us in a conscious way through the day,
making observations of our own impatient reactions as we
try to build in the new quality.

101

The word "patience" comes from the Latin *pati*, meaning "to suffer." A definition of patience is "the suffering or enduring of pain, trouble, or evil with calmness and composure."

Several other qualities of the heart are closely related to patience. In order to remove oneself from solar plexus suffering and agitation, *detachment* is required. In the process we may very well need to exercise *tolerance*. Patience, like tolerance, requires a calm standing by, a waiting, while some form of "trouble" is occurring. The reason one can calmly stand by is that one *identifies* or endeavors to identify with the soul within, which is recognized here as something that *persists* down the ages and has continuity or *immortality*.

The keywords for P.D.W. (rays II, 6, 5-5-7) are Patience, Dynamic thought, and Wisdom, as we see in the following paragraph:

> Like our Great Master the Christ, you must and do shoulder your share of the world suffering, thereby forming one of the great group of His companions who are pledged to the "fellowship of His sufferings and His patience," as He is pledged to His great Master, the Lord of Shamballa. He, as you know, will not leave His post until the "last weary pilgrim has found his way home." You see, therefore, do you not, the true significance of the three keywords which I gave you when you entered this group---endless *patience*, with yourself, with others and with erring humanity; *dynamic thought*, giving you power and usefulness upon the mental plane and teaching you to work there as does the Christ, as does K.H. and all who are serving in connection

with the Hierarchy; *wisdom*, enabling you to reap the fruitage of many lives, spent in acquiring spiritual knowledge.
Discipleship in the New Age, v.1, pp. 438-9.

The sixth ray of idealism and devotion, conditioning the astral body and the personality, brings in both an acute sensitivity to suffering on the emotional plane and a ray relationship with Christ (the second and the sixth rays bring about that possible connection).

The keynotes here seem to relate directly to his psychological ray equipment. The keyword of Wisdom clearly draws upon the second ray soul energy. The keyword of Patience tends to still somewhat the devotional intensity of the sixth ray and quiet the sixth ray stimulation of the solar plexus center. The keyword of Dynamic Thought and the urge to work upon the mental plane augments the fifth ray conditioning the mind and may also bring in something of the first ray of power via the 1-3-5 connection.

P.D.W. was a Frenchman and ex-Jesuit priest who died in Holland during the Second World War. The Great Master, the Christ, was held up to him as a perfect manifestation of patience. Attention was drawn to the factor of suffering and the shouldering of world pain. In the development of patience, the feelings of pain and suffering are not so much avoided as endured, endured as necessary factors in the awakening of consciousness and the Christ aspect. P.D.W. was called upon to be patient and to suffer in that world and Christ-like sense, but not to anguish emotionally. The latter would tend to deplete one of needed energy.

Short Review on Patience.

1. Was I able to substitute patience for hurry?
   For irritability?
2. Was I impatient, wanting immediate results?
   If so, what were the results?
   Or was I patient, and what was its effect?
3. What triggers impatience for me?
   Am I too concerned with form?
   Can I be patient with budding consciousness?
   And is it a joy to be so?
4. Three qualities greatly appreciated by most everyone
   are love, patience, and understanding. Was I able
   to bring these qualities into the environment today?
5. "The suffering of the soul, when the personality goes
   astray, is only a symbolic form of words. There is
   no pain or true suffering, and frequently no knowledge of the happening, for the vibration is not high
   enough to penetrate into that high place where dwells
   the soul. Where, however, there is such knowledge,
   the soul experiences, if I might so express it, a sense
   of lost opportunity, and therefore a sense of frustration,
   but it is not more than that, for the patience of the soul,
   as of the Hierarchy, is illimitable. Just because we
   speak symbolically and say the soul suffers, you must
   not interpret it in ordinary terms.

   "The suffering of Christ or of the planetary Logos
   or of God Himself, is not comprehensible in terms of
   personality reaction." *Esoteric Healing*, pp. 346-7.

   Was I able to approach the "illimitable patience
   of the soul" today?

Tolerance is the First Expression of Buddhic Understanding. Exoteric definitions of tolerance include:

- Capacity to endure.
- Sympathy or indulgence for beliefs or practices differing from or conflicting with one's own.
- The allowable deviation from a standard.
- Suffering of something to be or to be done without prohibition, hindrance or contradiction.

One of the differences between tolerance and identification is that with identification one comes to understand a person or a situation in a very deep way. One comes to understand something that is different or other than one self. Only the heart is able to make the deep-level discernment. One's own life is broadened and expanded to include and to embrace the other. With tolerance it is not a matter of expanding to a point of being able to identify, for here there already is a good understanding of the person or situation. It is not a matter of understanding a foreign situation, for one already *knows* the situation. It is rather a matter of not saying anything or doing anything to correct it (not "prohibiting, hindering, or contradicting"). From the definitions above, one "endures" the wrong, one "suffers" the known deviation.

Why would one do that, and how is tolerance the "first expression of buddhic understanding"?

Generally and basically, if one corrects another--- externally, as it were---it is seldom as thorough and as comprehensive a learning experience as is self-correction and self-discovery. Self-correction has to do with an internal recognition and subsequent right action. In a certain sense, one could say that life is a better teacher than you or I.

Also, correcting another often has to do with *projecting rather than knowing*.

Looking at it from a slightly different angle, one could say that wisdom (the heart) grants freedom. We do not want to deprive a person of a certain amount of freedom (liberty), even when there is deviation from certain accepted norms or when there is conflict with some of our cherished ideas, opinions, and patterns, for we do not want to deprive a person of a potentially enriching or learning experience.

One must remember, of course, that all the virtues and keynotes speak of a balanced middle path and not of extremes. We do not play into the hands of evil by tolerating gross corruption. There is always a ring-pass-not and thus-far-and-no-further. So, finding a right balance, one is neither intolerant (not an overly strict advocate of some supposed standard of perfection), nor permissive to the point of excessive disorder and harmfulness.

Tolerance has to do with a trust in the basic goodness of humankind. We are speaking of a quality of the heart. One might say that only the heart knows of the deep and often hidden underlying goodness of humankind. Where there is no tolerance, and where there is a forced compliance of one's own vision of the good, there is often no true vision. History teems with examples of major mistakes of religious and political intolerance.

Tolerance has to do with "knowing the end from the beginning." Most "beginnings," in this sense, have to do with stages of development, and therefore cannot be whole, complete, right, and perfect. Right development only occurs when there is room for experiment and experience.

This brings us to the peculiarities of the human family in contradistinction to the instinctual rightness of other kingdoms in nature. The fourth ray of harmony through conflict is one of the major rays conditioning humanity. Conflict, and therefore deviation, is built into the system. Interestingly, the fourth ray is also the major ray of the buddhic plane, the plane of intuition and pure reason. In a certain sense one could say that certain ray energies are better for teaching and for education than are other rays. In this day and age the second ray of love-wisdom, the third ray of active intelligence, and the fifth ray of science play an important role in education. One could also say that an important ray for learning the hard way, learning primarily through experience, learning the *art* of something, is the fourth ray of harmony through conflict. Here we get into a realm where verbal communication (as in intelligence and science) plays less of a direct role. The art of something cannot be directly taught but only emerges after long periods of experiment and experience. Tolerance plays into that type of learning and experience.

In a certain sense then humanity has a greater degree of freedom, a greater leeway of experimentation, that enables it, in designed or destined fashion, to learn---albeit in a difficult manner, accompanied by much pain and suffering. What is humanity learning? Humanity is probably learning to become co-creators with God. Christ said: *Do ye not know that ye are gods?* Man often appears to be the most un-god-like creature in God's universe. God's tolerance for deviation here is great.

The kingdom in nature that is responsible (in an immediate and direct sense) for human evolution is the next higher kingdom. The Masters of Wisdom, we are told, are focused in buddhic consciousness. Since this is higher than the plane of soul, we might imagine it as being a ray energy that has not the conflicts and distortions of fourth ray energy visible in the human kingdom. We would find here then an exquisite play of sound and color that is used in the orchestration of form creation (as in thought-form building) that gives expression to the Life and Purpose of Deity. The fourth plane of buddhi bridges between the higher three and the lower three. There is a creative expression involved here, and there is also "the Corrector of the Form, the Trumpet of the Lord, and the Divine Intermediary." One of the aphorisms of the Fourth ray is:

> Color the sound. Sound forth the color.
> Produce the notes and see them pass
> into the shades, which in their turn
> produce the sounds.
> Thus all are seen as one.
> Quality..........the synthesis of true beauty.
> *Esoteric Psychology*, v.1, p.72.

In spite of the "shades" and shadows---which one tolerates and even suffers gladly, as it were---"all are seen as one."

Both the second ray of love (conditioning the heart) and the fourth ray of harmony and beauty enable us to appreciate in some degree the overtones of the virtue of tolerance.

We might ask ourselves, which ray types find the virtue of tolerance most difficult to embody? It seems that the first ray of power and the sixth ray of idealism, as they play through the distorting tendencies of the personal consciousness, could prove somewhat problematical for this virtue of the heart. As mentioned, these two rays played prominently in D.H.B.'s psychological equipment and were the very reason why meditations on the twelve qualities of the heart were suggested.

The Twelfth Quality. We have discussed briefly three of the eleven qualities of the heart given by D.K. Some speculate as to what the twelfth quality could be. The quality that comes to my mind as a link with the heart and a link with the Christ is *forgiveness*.

Forgiveness means "to give" and it also means "to cease to feel resentment against an offender." The word is included in the Lord's Prayer. It is contained in Christ's teachings on love, which includes among other things, "turning the other cheek." It is the new law and the *New Testament* substitute for the old eye-for-an-eye principle. It is a word that was uttered by Christ on the cross.

Without forgiveness it seems that there is no escape from the lesser cycles and the rotary, self-centered motion. Forgiveness seems to break or enable one to stand free of Saturn's Law.

Short Review on Forgiveness.
1. What "debt" or "trespass" am I capable of forgiving? Can I forgive the large and the small?
2. As I briefly scan my early years, do I find any hidden or repressed resentments that I need to bring forth and resolve? Can I say with a heart full of love and understanding, "I forgive you, and I bless you on your spiritual way"?
3. Forgiving someone and asking forgiveness (apologizing) are two sides of the same coin. Do I need to ask someone for forgiveness? Do I need to apologize to someone? Do I have the strength to do this?
4. Can a take a particular resentment that I carry with me in my aura and loosen its hold on me? Can I find release through the forgiveness of a

loving heart?
5. Can we say *from our hearts* as Christ said on
   the Cross, "Forgive them; they know not what
   they do."
   At the same time, however, are we sure we *know*
   what we do?
7. Can I imagine what a forgiving world would be
   like? Can I help build such a world?

Meditation on Gratitude and Forgiveness.
There are a great many things to be thankful for.
Gratitude kindles quickly the energies of the heart.

Stage I: Quiet and relax the physical body. Take
   a few deep breaths bringing energy and relaxation
   to the physical body, quieting the emotions, and
   bringing a peaceful alertness to the mind.

Stage II: Meditate on the quality of gratitude.
   Is there someone who has helped us recently or in
   the past. Is there someone who has been trying to
   help us and we have failed to accept their heart-felt
   aid? Is there someone on the inner side who has been
   giving us guidance and blessing? With a heart full of
   love we accept this great gift. With all gratitude we
   accept this spiritually connecting gift.
   "Ponder upon the treasures which are given to us and
   which belong to the One who brought us a tear and a
   drop of sweat for our liberation. Let us also daily thank
   the Highest One." *Hierarchy*, 177.
   "He who has found the seed and realized the care of the
   Sender can project gratitude into the space. Great is the

healing power of the emission of gratitude."
Agni Yoga, 31.

Stage III: Within the spirit of gratitude and with a heart full
of love, we extend forgiveness, mercy, and compassion
out onto the world.
"In each life one finds many occasions for malice; to accumulate them throughout one's lives would create a long
black tail that drags and impedes. With such an appen-
dage one cannot advance!"   *Supermundane,* v.1, 75.

With our mind's eye we scan the short and long past. Are
there any points of resentment, for apparent wrongs done
to us, from which we need release?
In the spirit of gratitude for the good in the inner and
outer worlds, we say with a heart full of love, I forgive
you...and I bless you...on your spiritual path.

"Mercy is measured not so much in so-called good actions, the cause of which can be too varied, but by the in-
most kindliness; it kindles the light which shines in the
darkness."   *Heart,* 7.

Stage IV: Close with the affirmation:
"In the center of all love I stand.
From that center I the soul will outward move.
From that center I the one who serves will work.
May the love of the Divine Self be shed abroad in my
heart, through my group, and throughout the world."

D.K. Takes Forgiveness an Octave Higher. "The recognition of the faculty of forgiveness is, or rather should be, the expression of the relationship between unit and unit within the larger group, or of group and group within the larger whole. Forgiveness is essentially the process whereby each gives to each along psychical lines, and it is one of the rudimentary expressions of the quality of self-sacrifice which is , in its turn, an aspect of the will nature of Deity. Being therefore related to the monadic or will life, it is as yet completely misunderstood and misinterpreted. It is in reality the sense of synthesis or of identification and of 'each for all and all for each.' This sense is being developed today as never before, but it is still so embryonic that words do not help in explaining it. This faculty of forgiveness is not a form of magnanimous forgetting or overlooking, neither is it a gesture of superiority whereby the slate is wiped clean. It is the very breath of life itself---the giving of all to all and for all." *Education in the New Age*, p. 129.

Methods for Finding One's
Own Keywords

Method One: The Keyword via the Dream. This method
can be approached in two different ways:
1. *Directly and from suggestion.*
   With this method one makes the focused and
concentrated suggestion to oneself before going
to sleep that one will either have a dream that
will symbolically reveal the keyword or words,
or, if there is no dream, that the keywords will
be clear to one upon awakening.
   One uses this technique in something of a
ritualistic way. Before going to sleep one reads
something about the keywords. One reflects on
the keywords without selecting any. One may
light a candle or do something that increases a
certain solemnity. Then one puts the suggestion
or request to the soul, and to those who guide
humanity from the inner side, that upon awakening one's keywords will be clear to one.
   Upon awakening it is important to quietly
recall the previous evening's request, and then
let the words come. Simply that.

2. *Via the symbolic dream, when it occurs.*

When one has what seems to be a deeply meaningful dream that demands recording and interpreting, then usually a keyword of significance can be extracted from it.

In the preceding chapters we have interpreted three dreams, which dramatized the need to *reach out* to others, the need for *rest (the need for green)*, and the need to *include the qualities of the nun*, or *hold the inner spiritual conference*, or simply *confer*.

What is required here is some skill in interpreting dreams and reading symbols. Even if one thinks one does not have these skills, nevertheless, if one writes the dream down and spends some thought time on the project, the meaning may gradually surface.

It is important to realize that generally the dream *externalizes* or pictures forth the inner characteristics. No matter how much we dislike certain things in our dreams, these "things" are most often unrecognized aspects of ourselves. We tend not to see ourselves, and often the only hope of seeing ourselves is when we see ourselves in others. Life then has a way of mirroring ourselves back to us. In the dream, generally, we play in the world we have created in consciousness.

Method Two: The Opening of the Book.
Some people seem to have success with this method. It entails the use of a spiritual book as a sort of oracle. One would select a specific book and, after alignment and meditative thinking on the matter, one would open the book

with closed eyes and place a finger on the Word.

If one draws a blank page, this method is not for you. This method should not be trivialized through too frequent use.

Method Three: The Keyword Via Meditation or Meditative Reflection on the Keywords.
This method is simply spiritual or esoteric study, followed by reflective thought. One needs to be academically familiar with the whole subject matter of keywords as it is employed in esoteric psychology. This purpose of this book, as stated, is to elucidate this process.

In some ways this is a trial-and-error method---an experimental process. One must be aware of the tricks the personality plays on one. The keyword we think is ours, may simply be a glamorous notion of ours. The keyword we do not want to have, may very well be ours.

The keyword can come from a variety of sources, or rather, the source as the soul, the keywords can come along a variety of avenues. The keyword always indicates *work.* We can be alert to *signs* that can indicate or confirm a particular keyword.

Method Four: The Keyword via the Esoteric Psychologist. One might say that this is a non-paid profession. D.K. mentions that what is needed now-a-days is experts in the life of the soul. The horoscope of a person can sometimes be helpful, if one see it within its present limitations.

As the esotercist studies the three aspects of the new science of psychology---the rays, the chakras, and esoteric astrology---she or he will be able to help others through the profound simplicity of the keywords. The esoteric psychologist has a working knowledge of the soul and sees all development in light of unfolding the soul within. Instead of working primarily with symptoms and with the goal of normalcy or conformity or compliance, the esoteric psychologist will look at energy development, balance, and alignment. She or he will look for the non-physical causes rather than tinkering with effects.

The Keyword from the Master. This is possible, of course, but nothing need be said about it.

"Through culture and the realization of goal-fitness the great concept of the Teacher is formed. To realize the significance of the conception of the Teacher will constitute the passing through the first gates of evolution. One should not bring into the concept of the Teacher supermundane preconceptions. He should be the One Who gives the best advice in life. This practicality will embrace Knowledge, Creation and Infinity."   *Agni Yoga*, para. 43.

Summary and Further Research Aids

Brief Summary of the Major Principles.
At the heart of the right use of keywords or keynotes, as a means of aligning and blending with the soul or higher self, are the principles of *simplicity* and *profundity*. Profundity simply means reaching within to the next higher level of consciousness---a level of greater *refinement* and *expansiveness* of vibration. This approach is accompanied by a certain *solemnity*. Three keywords here would be *seriousness, sacredness,* and something done in the *silence* of one's own heart.

The personality and the intellect tend to fall into the "trap of many words." The right use of keywords endeavors to avoid this tendency. The intellectual personality can go through extensive mental gymnastics in an effort to perpetuate its glamours and illusions---its subtle and not so subtle addictions, as it were. In the *recognition* of this lesser self, and in its steady *waning,* the true Self can *"grow and glow."*

Determining the correct keyword is both a science and a great art. Aids to the science of it include:

1. An understanding of the seven ray energies.

117

2. Recognition of the subtle bodies:
   - the soul or higher self (transpersonal)
   - the personality (temporary and
     self-centered)
   - the three aspects of personality:
     - mind, intellect, lower concrete mind
     - emotion, sentience, feeling
     - physical-etheric (the vital or energy
       puls the dense physical)
3. Esoteric Astrology.

Aids to the art of it include:

1. Being able to determine or having a workable
   hypothesis as to the ray equipment---which rays
   are conditioning which vehicles (subtle bodies).
2. Knowing or having a good estimate of the assets
   and debits of the particular ray equipment.
   Which rays in the individual are developed.
   Which rays are lacking. How can the ray
   energies be brought into right unfoldment and
   right balance.
3. What is the next step ahead. What keyword or
   words can be used to facilitate the next step
   ahead.

The keywords are forms---word forms or thought
forms---that embody energy. Thus, they are vital, real, and
dynamic. These word energies are attributes of soul, they
are qualities of the soul. As such, they lead one to soul.
They render the personality harmless and enable it to be a
vehicle for the soul energies.

Work is required in order to build in these energies.
The work includes study, clear definition, meditation,
reflection or review work, and much application. The work

118

requires the long term view. This is not work that can be accomplished on a weekend or in two weeks. The work is in the daily and monthly cycles. It requires a six month view that extends to a year. It requires a cycle of seven years. It requires a life-time.

The soul's purpose is always *to serve* one's brothers. The energy, since it relates to the greater Reality, is always *intensely practical.*

In this final chapter we include a brief look at some other keywords used in *Discipleship in the New Age.*

Responsibility. If we think of responsibility from a soul or more spiritual angle, then we realize that we have spiritual as well as personal responsibilities. Meeting our personal responsibilities to family is, of course, most necessary. Christ said: "Seek ye first the kingdom of heaven and all these things shall be added on to you." Our personal responsibilities and duties can work out *rightly* when they are in or under the larger perspective of our group or soul responsibilities.

Responsibility is another one of those keywords that most everyone needs to reflect upon. It involves also the recognition of *karma* and relates to the right use of *time.*

"One's spiritual responsibility is, curiously enough, usually the last to be recognized, and action taken on that responsibility is usually slow. Yet, in the last analysis, it is by far the most important, for one's spiritual influences can be lasting and can carry with it releasing power to those we love, whereas the other responsibility---being those of personality relationships---always carry with them glamour and that which is not of the kingdom of the spirit."

Discipleship in the New Age, v.1, p. 518.

Comradeship. Being a brother to a brother, working as co-workers in a spirit of mutual support and non-criticism, is no easy task. Personalities compete with one another and self-love is strong.

The personal sense of self can be forgotten, however, in the process of shared work, as D.K. points out:

"The sense of comradeship is surely known by each and all of you but needs the deepening of service shared. Show this and draw it forth. The comradeship of burdens shared, the sense of deep response to need, the comradeship of service rendered, the urge to sacrifice---teach these to those who seek to work within the Master's plan and show all three yourself." (p. 167)

"Comradeship . . . is not an easy lesson at any time for first ray souls to master and express. The littleness of the personalities and the pettiness of individual points of view are irksome to the server of the Plan who stands, serene and detached, upon a first ray pinnacle of vision and resultant comprehension." (p. 169)

Sacrifice. It seems to me that this is a keyword with which every serious student is well acquainted. It is probably a keyword, however, that one would only reluctantly chose as having special significance for oneself. Like many of the keywords most of us would probably do well in trying to discern some of the deeper implications of sacrifice. D.K. gives us a hint for meditative work and thoughtful consideration:

"The sense of sacrifice is faintly seen in every soul that loves the Plan. Teach them that sacrifice must touch the depths of giving and not call forth that which upon the surface lies or that which can be known. The unseen

sacrifice must go with that which can be seen. Teach this."
(p. 167)

Leadership. Leadership is clearly a most important factor.
All aspirants look for the teacher or for the one further
along on a Path that they someday will have to go. Disciples also look for a true leader. At the same time, all are
rightfully suspicious of anyone who assumes any kind of
leadership role. All are reluctant to be lead. Ultimately, we
are led from within, which at one level is the soul. Yet this
"individuality" is not individually focused.

D.K. gives us four lessons of leadership.

1. The first has to do with the "lesson of vision."
   The leader always has a vision. Is this a personal
   vision? One in which the leader sees him/herself
   at the center of some organization? "What is the
   spiritual incentive which will be and is strong
   enough to hold you steady to the purpose and
   true to the objective? No one can formulate the
   vision for you; it is your personality problem, and
   upon the strength of the vision and the beauty of
   the picture which you paint with your imagination
   will depend much that you do and become."

2. The second lesson D.K. calls the development of
   the "right sense of proportion." This had to do
   with *humility*. "No true leader can be anything
   but humble, for he realizes the magnitude of his
   task; he appreciates the limitations of his contribution (in the light of the vision) and the need for
   constant self-development and the cultivation of
   the spirit of steady inner spiritual learning, if he is
   ever to make his proper contribution."

3. The third lesson has to do with the development

121

of the spirit of synthesis. "This enables you to include all within the range of your influence and also to be included within the range of those greater than yourself. Thus is the chain of Hierarchy established."

4. Another lesson has to do with the "avoidance of the spirit of criticism, for criticism leads to barriers and the loss of time. Learn to distinguish the spirit of criticism from the ability to analyze and make practical application of the analysis. Learn to analyze life, circumstances and people from the angle of the work, and not from the angle of your personality point of view...."
Discipleship in the New Age, v.2, p. 704.

Simplicity. "The simplicity of the soul opens the way into Shamballa.... Of the group which finds its way into Shamballa a developed simplicity will be found to govern all relations."

"Simplicity and unity are related; simplicity is one-pointedness of outlook, free from glamour and the intricacies of the thoughtform-making mind; simplicity is clarity of purpose and steadfastness in intention and in effort, untrammelled by questioning and devious introspection; simplicity leads to simple loving, asking nothing in return; simplicity leads to silence---not silence as an escape mechanism, but as an occult retention of speech." (Volume 2, pp. 518-519.)

Purification. In the work of purification, D.K. emphasizes the utilization of the *technique of substitution*. Instead of combating the impure, he suggests substituting "dynamic good thoughts" as a means of correcting "wrong thought habits."

D.K. gave S.R.D. a series of six seed thoughts for meditation, each to be used for the duration of a month:

1....The purification of the astral body.
2....The purification of the physical body.
3....The means whereby the brain can be rendered sensitive to the higher impressions.
4....The elimination of those habits which tend to cloud the mind and render the man insensitive to the higher contact.
5....The nature of purification from the angle of the vision of the disciple.
6....The formulation of those disciplines which will aid in purification.

"If you will do this faithfully, in six months it will be apparent to you why I have stressed this aspect of the training in your life and work." (Vol. 1, p. 569.)

Courage. *"Above everything else, I wish you were more courageous."* This was written not to a single disciple but to all of them. "It takes courage to make spiritual decisions and to abide by the; it takes courage to adjust your lives--- daily and in all relations---to the need of the hour and to the service of mankind; it takes courage to demonstrate to those around you that the present world catastrophe is of more importance to you than the petty affairs of your individual lives and your humdrum contacts; it takes courage to dis- card the alibis which have prevented you from participating to date in the all-out effort which characterizes today the ac- tivities of the Hierarchy; it takes courage to make sacrifices, to refuse time to nonessential activities. . . it takes courage to attack life on behalf of others, and to obliterate your own wishes in the emergency and need."
Discipleship in the New Age, v 2, pp. 42-3.

Group Understanding. It seems to me that one of the most significant---and also one of the most difficult---factors in this work is *group* consciousness and *group* work. I think it would be a fitting place to conclude this brief study of *Discipleship in the New Age* with a few thought provoking quotes from D.K. on this all important subject.

"In this group work you will need to remember that increasingly there will be no *individual* life. This is as it should be. Increasingly disciples should be aware of each other and tune in with ease on each other; increasingly the bonds of illumined loyalty should control; increasingly you will participate in each other's attitudes and conditions and thus learn the basic lesson of understanding. Understanding is the secret behind all power to achieve identification with any form of divine expression; understanding is one of the prime factors in producing revelation, and this is one of the paradoxes of occultism. In the world of human thought, understanding follows the prescribed routine, it follows the presented fact. In the life of the spirit, understanding is a necessary predisposing *cause of revelation.*"
*(D.N.A.,v.2,*p.14.)

In this letter to the group D.K. goes on to discuss the individual need to have a deep understanding of the initiator within oneself and also the nature of the group work of approaching the Hierarchy during the time of the full moon. Understanding plays a key role as a "predisposing" factor. The specific group work that D.K. outlines here is that of the full moon approach to Hierarchy. "Pour out love to each of the group members," he suggests, as you link up as a group.

124

Group Unity, Love, and the Heart Center. "Our immediate concern is a bringing about a group unity rooted in love, and this requires the awakening of the heart center into greater potency.... Only from the heart can stream, in reality, those lines of energy which link and bind together....This heart center, when adequately radiatory and magnetic, will relate you afresh to each other and to all the world.... The activity of the heart center *never* demonstrates in connection with individuals. This is a basic fact. What devastates most disciples is the solar plexus ability (when purified and consecrated) to identify itself with individuals. The heart center cannot react, except under group impetus, group happiness or unhappiness, and other group relations." (*D.N.A.,v.2*, pp.113,114.)

Only from the heart center can we find those energies which bind and link. Often we think that if we sufficiently clarify something---working from the throat center---that the group will then come together more closely, but that is not the case. Love is more foundational here than light. Sometimes, or at a certain stage, there is a tendency to work at gathering knowledge and bringing light, but there is the failure to work sufficiently at quickening the heart center.

The solar plexus center can greatly interfere with the right unfoldment of the heart center and true group work. Here we have emotionalism of one sort or another. The heart can greatly help other people with their temporary lapses into the clouds of emotion.
Being critical of them and judging them would be worse than trying to assimilate them into the group.

"I would like here to emphasize one point as we consider the individual in the group and his group relations. Watch with care your thoughts anent each other, and kill out at once all suspicion, all criticism and seek to hold each other unwaveringly in the light of love. You have no idea of the potency of such an effort or of the power to release each other's bonds and to lift the group to an exceedingly high place. By the pure light of love for each other, you can draw nearer to me and to the teachers on the subjective side of life and arrive more rapidly at that Gate which opens on the lighted Way." (*D.N.A.,v.1*,p.10.)

The Wrong Kind of Indifference.   "A deep reflection upon the urgency of the times and a sympathetic recognition of the unhappy plight of humanity are much needed by disciples and aspirants in the world today, particularly by those who are not close to the world situation but who are looking at it from a distance. It is so simple to give a facile expression of sympathy but at the same time to avoid too great an expenditure of energy in service and too intense an effort to be of assistance....

"If I were asked to specify the outstanding fault of the majority of groups of disciples at this time, I would say that it is the expression of the wrong kind of indifference, leading to an almost immovable pre-occupation with their personal ideas and undertakings. These
 militate against the group integration and tend to block the work.

"One of the things most needed by every disciple is to apply the teaching given to the idea of promoting and increasing their world service, thus rendering practical and effective in their environment the knowledge that has been imparted and the stimulation to which they have been subjected. This is a suggestion to which I would have you pay real attention." (*D.N.A.,v.1*,pp. 82, 83.)

Group Steadiness and the Freedom from Oscillation.
"This grows out of right integration and refers to the
delicate balance which must be preserved amongst the
members of the group. This is of such a nature that there
emerges eventually a group steadiness and a group freedom
from 'oscillation' which will permit of uninterrupted group
work and interplay. It will come if each of the group
members will simply mind his own business and permit his
group brothers to mind theirs; it will come if you keep your
personality affairs, your private concerns and troubles out of
the group life; it will come if you refrain from discussion of
each other and of each other's affairs and attitudes. This is
of supreme importance at this stage of the group work; it
will mean---if you can achieve success in this---that you will
be able to keep your minds clear of all lesser things which
concern the personality life. This means that your minds
will be free, therefore, for group work." (*D.N.A., v.1*, p.60.)

Groups in the Next Cycle. "The externalized groups of
disciples are all of them intended to be expressions of a type
of group relation which will be better known and
understood when the world has entered into the next cycle
and era of peace. Certain types of force are to be later
utilized by the groups for specific group ends and for world
service... The fact that one group will work with one type of
force and another group of disciples will employ a different
kind must not in any sense be deemed to indicate separate
activity or separative interests. All will be working towards
one objective or goal and all will work with the same divine
energy, differentiated into varying forces for the purpose of
service in one department of life or another." (*Disc. New
Age*, v.1, pp. 67-68.)

APPENDIX

The Seven Rays

Definitions of the Seven Ray Energies.
"There is one Life, which expresses Itself primarily through seven basic qualities or aspects, and secondarily through the myriad diversity of forms.

"These seven radiant qualities are the seven Rays, the seven Lives, who give Their life to the forms, and give the form world its meaning, its laws, and its urge to evolution.

"Life, quality and appearance, or spirit, soul and body constitute all that exists. They are existence itself, with its capacity for growth, for activity, for manifestation of beauty, and for full conformity to the Plan. This Plan is rooted in the consciousness of the seven ray Lives...." (See: *Treatise on the Seven Rays, v.1*, pp. 141-143.)

The Names of the Seven Rays.
 I. The First Ray of Will or Power.
 II. The Second Ray of Love-Wisdom.
 III. The Third Ray of Intelligent Activity.
 IV. The Fourth Ray of Harmony Through Conflict.
 V. The Fifth Ray of Scientific Knowledge.
 VI. The Sixth Ray of Idealism and Devotion.
 VII. The Seventh Ray of Organization or
    Ceremonial Magic.

The Three Aspects of Spirit, Soul, and Body (Personality).

1. Monad...........Spirit.......1st Aspect..........Will...............Purpose
2. Egoic Lotus.....Soul........2nd Aspect.....Consciousness......Quality
3. Personality......Body......3rd Aspect.......Activity........Adaptability
                                                              Intelligence

The Three Aspects of the Soul or the Egoic Lotus.
1. The Sacrificial Petals...relating to Atma, the spiritual will.
2. The Love Petals.........relating to Buddhi, or the intuition.
3. The Knowledge Petals........relating to Manas, or higher
                                                     abstract mind.

These three aspects of the soul are also called:
Conscious Will, Conscious Love, and Conscious Activity.

The Three Aspects of Personality.
1. The mental body...............lower concrete mind................thought.
2. The emotional body.............feeling, sentience....................desire.
3. The physical-etheric body.....dense form - prana...............activity.

The Rays of Soul and Personality.
The soul can be on anyone of the seven rays. The soul ray remains the same through a world period.

The personality (the soul's vehicle of manifestation) can be on any one of the seven rays. The soul ray stays the same, generally speaking; the personality ray changes from life to life. The ray of the personality can be seen as a sub-ray of the soul ray. The sub-rays round out the experience of the soul, making it comprehensive, balanced, and whole.

The mental body is generally on either ray 1, 4, or 5:
        1: the administrative-responsible mind,
        4: the creative-artistic mind,
        5: the defining-observing-scientific mind.
The emotion-astral body is generally on either ray 2 or 6.
The physical body (including brain) is generally on either ray 3 or 7

There is a correspondence to be noted here in the bodies
and the planes.

        Physical plane............................seventh ray
        Emotional plane.........................sixth ray
        Mental plane..............................fifth ray
        Buddhic plane.............................fourth ray
        Atmic plane................................third ray
        Monadic plane............................second ray
        Adi...first ray

        The 6th ray astral body sorts out much in terms of
likes-dislikes, pain and pleasure, swinging between the pairs
of opposites,   and functioning under the law of attraction
and repulsion. Feelings are often intense and often confused
as intense liking can revert to intense disliking. Devotion of
the 6th ray can become fanaticism, when unbalanced by
other ray development. The 2nd ray astral body is calmer
and more inclusive, generally speaking.
        The 3rd ray physical body is generally more ener-
getic, more active, more robust, than the more delicate,
rhythm oriented, ritual loving 7th ray physical.
        The three types of mind---1st ray, 4th ray, and 5th
ray---are most interesting at this stage of racial history and
evolutionary development. They look, one might say, in
three different directions.

The 4th ray type is either looking to the feeling-emotional plane or towards the intuitive buddhic plane. Creativity and beauty and sensitivity are keywords here.

The 1st ray mind tends towards issues of responsibility, control, power, "handling men and measures," and administrative and legal matters. Orderly relationships are a concern here, as are often discipline, self-control and perfect poise. One can see that the eye here is not on the emotional plane but on the physical plane. This mind can bring in a detaching, impersonal demeanor--- negatively, cold, somewhat harsh, positively, strong and reliable.

The 5th ray mind is most at home on the 5th plane of mind. Detachment, reasoning, observing are keywords here. The 5th ray mind tends not to jump to conclusions, tends to be very cautious about judgment. This type of mind tends to be somewhat skeptical. This type likes to specialize, to delve deeply into matters, to master a field of knowledge. Knowledge is a keyword here.

The Rays and Lines of Energy.
There are certain energy flows, relationships, that could be called paths of least resistance.

Rays one-three-five-and seven find a certain compatible interplay. These are the rays of concretion.

Rays two-four-six find a certain complementary relationship. These are the rays of abstraction.

The necessity yet danger of form manifestation has to do with separation. Too much form orientation and concretion can lead to excess density and materialism. Too much other-worldly abstraction can lead to an ephemeral loose connection and non-vital relationship. The two sets of rays and energy lines require each other in order to off-set

131

the Law of Separation. One can look at things concrete with a spiritual eye; one can look at such abstractions as consciousness, beauty, religion, and deity with a scientific eye, and in the process balance the pairs of opposites and become an occultist in the true and original meaning of that term.

The Book *Discipleship in the New Age.*
I would ask you to take the new book, Disciple-ship in the New Age, *and each day meditate upon its significance, its usefulness and its teaching value in this coming post-war period. read it carefully, even when you know much of what is said; build a thoughtform of the book and see it going forth to the very ends of the Earth. this book, if rightly distributed, can act as a great magnet, drawing people from all over the planet into the Ashrams of the Masters, and thereby increasing the potency of the workers for humanity as well as increasing them numer-ically.*

Excerpt from a letter to R.V.B., *Discipleship in the New Age*, v. 2, p. 559.

Pythagoras's Evening Review. The students of Pathagoras's community were required, at the close of each day, to ask themselves three questions:
1. What wrongs have I committed?
2. What duties have I neglected?
3. What good have I done?

Bibliography

Abraham, Kurt. *Balancing the Pairs of Opposites; The Seven Rays and Education; and Other Essays in Esoteric Psychology.* White City, Oregon: Lampus Press, 1993

Agni Yoga. New York: Agni Yoga Society, 1929.

Bailey, Alice A. *Discipleship in the New Age,* v. 1-2. New York: Lucis Publishing, 1944, 1955.

-------*Education in the New Age.* NY: Lucis, 1954.

-------*Esoteric Astrology.* NY: Lucis, 1951.

-------*Esoteric Healing.* NY: Lucis, 1953.

-------*Esoteric Psychology.* NY: Lucis, 1942.

-------*Glamour: A World Problem.* NY: Lucis, 1950.

-------*Telepathy and the Etheric Vehicle.* NY: Lucis 1950.

-------*Rays and the Initiations.* NY: Lucis, 1960.

-------*Treatise on Cosmic Fire.* NY: Lucis, 1925.

-------*Treatise on White Magic.* NY: Lucis, 1934.

Durant, Will. *The Life of Greece.* New York: Simon and Schuster, 1939.

Fiery World, vol. 1. New York: Agni Yoga Society, 1933.

Heart. New York: Agni Yoga Society, 1932.

Hierarchy. New York: Agni Yoga Society, 1931.

Infinity, v. 2. New York: Agni Yoga Society, 1930.

Leaves of Morya's Garden. New York: Agni Yoga Society, 1925.

Supermundane, The Inner Life, v.2. New York: Agni Yoga Society, 1938.

Index

A

Abstraction, 87, 131-2
Action, 40, 62
Activity, 41, 43, 47, 50, 60, 80, 86
Adaptability, 129
Adrenals, 81
Adi, 130
Air, 39, 41
Ajna center, 20, 81
Alchemical, 90
Aloofness, 29
Anger, 30
Appearance, 128
Arhat, 16, 17
Arhatship, 91
Aries, 39
Art, 49, 107, 117
Ashram, 47, 63, 65, 89, 132
Aspiration, 15, 72-3
Aspirant, 61, 63
Astral, 14, 27, 57, 76, 130
Astrology, 24, 115, 118
Atmic, 130
Atom, atomic, 82-3, 86-8
Attachment, 18-20, 22, 25, 27, 29, 31, 32, 56
Attention, 65
Attractive (magnetic), 89
Aura, 29, 81

B

Bailey, Alice, 3

Balance, 4, 5, 8, 9, 41, 56, 59, 60, 106, 116, 118
Base of spine center, 20, 81, 83
Beauty, 7, 8-17, 42, 74, 108, 131-2
Being, 58, 93
Benevolence, 16
Blame, 30
Blockage, 37
Blue, 14
Bodies, subtle, 5, 45, 118
Brahma, 85
Breath, 65-7
Bridge, 38-41, 108
Brother(s), 31, 120, 127
Buddhi, 108
Buddhic, 97, 100, 105, 107, 131
Buddha, 91
Building, 60
Business, 60

C

Catholic, 9
Cause(s), 65-6, 124
Centers, etheric, 81-2, 115
Ceremony, 12
Chela, 93
Christ, 9, 48, 56, 91, 102-4, 107, 109
Clarity, 3, 20, 30, 67
Color, 13, 14, 15, 42, 108

134

Communication, 60, 107
Compassion, 9,10, 37, 111
Comradeship, 120
Confidence, 39
Conservative, 41
Consciousness, 3, 19, 31, 38, 64, 67, 85-7, 108
Cosmos, 92
Courage, 123
Creation, 116
Creative, 12, 58, 108, 131
Crisis, 55, 66
Criticism, 53, 69, 120, 126
Crown chakra, 83
Culture, 116
Cycles, 55, 91, 119, 127
Cyclic, 62, 84-7

D
Danger, 39, 40
Decentralization, 23, 29, 44-54, 61, 91
Decision, 40, 45, 123
Deity, 48, 108, 132
Desire, 20, 31
Destiny, 61, 63
Destroy, 12
Destroyer, 87
Detachment, 18-32, 55-6, 61, 76, 93-4, 100-2, 131
Devotion, 9, 10
Dharma, 62-4
Diary, spiritual, 11, 13-14, 15
Differentiate, 61, 94
Disciple, 4, 27, 65, 80, 121, 127
Discriminative

Dispassion, 20
Divine, 49, 62, 108, 124
D.K., see Tibetan
Dream, 33-4, 36, 37, 38, 70-1, 113-14
Duality, 87
Dual life, 65
Duty, 62-5, 119, 132

E
Earth, 39-42, 85
Egoism, 63
Emotion, 14, 15, 20, 22, 24-5, 30, 39, 41-3, 45, 55, 65, 67, 77, 80, 101, 118, 125, 131
Emotionalism, 82, 125
Energy, 16, 65-6, 72, 82, 86, 107, 116, 126, 131
Esoteric, 3, 4, 16, 28, 44, 79, 115, 116, 118
Esotericism, 96
Essence, 82, 87-8, 98
Eternity, 29, 32
Evil, 16
Evolution, 62, 92, 116
Evolutionary arc, 86
Experience, 106-7
Experiment, 106-7
Express, 58
Extrovert, 44-7

F
Fear, 10, 31, 42
Fearlessness, 6, 39
Feeling, 12, 30, 35, 39-41, 43, 45, 57, 118

135

Fifth ray, 20, 23, 24, 26, 27, 101, 107, 128-132
Fire, 9, 16, 90, 92
· Fire by friction, 86
First ray, 8-12, 14, 15, 22, 24, 26-7, 29, 75, 77, 94, 95-6, 108, 128-132
Focus, 55, 61, 65-6
Forces, 24
Forgiveness, 109-12
Form, 29, 87-8, 99, 118
Fourth ray, 9, 11, 15, 21, 22, 42, 56, 67, 75-7, 106-7, 128-132
Freedom, 106-7, 127
Fusion, 98

G

Glamour, 4, 20, 26, 32, 60, 95, 100, 115, 117, 119, 122
Gland, 81
Goal, 60
Goal-fitness, 116
God, 46, 48, 107
Gold, 14
Golden, 28
Good, 16, 20, 61, 64, 132
Goodness, 106
Gonads, 81
Gratitude, 110-11
Green, 42, 114
Group, 4, 45, 47, 49, 63-4, 86, 97, 112, 124-7

H

Happy, 40
Happiness, 125

Head center, 98, see Crown chakra)
Healer, 91
Healing, 42, 83
Hierarchy, 17, 48, 89, 90, 103, 104, 122-4
Hints, 61, 67
Head, 10
Heart, 6, 10, 11, 12, 37, 44, 47, 48, 52, 53, 80-3, 93-112, 125
Heavenly Man, 83
Holy Spirit, 85
Homeopathy, 24
Human, 83
Humankind, 106
Humanity, 48, 68, 107, 126, 132
Humble, 71
Humility, 37, 53, 61, 72, 93-95, 97, 121

I

Identification, 10, 23, 37, 50, 56, 69, 87, 97-101, 105, 124
Individual, 124
Illumination, 62
Illusion, 44, 52, 60, 117
Imagination, 25, 50
Immortality, 101
Include, 73
Inclusiveness, 29
Indifference, 29-30, 91, 101, 126
Inertia, 43, 76. 86
Infinity, 116
Inhalation, 65-6
Inhibition, 15, 42
Initials, coded, 5

136

138

Pythagoras, 132

Q

Quality, 3, 4, 12, 16, 40, 68, 74, 99, 108-9, 128-9

R

Radiance, radiate, 7, 15, 42, 55, 58, 60, 75, 77, 79-80, 88, 91-92
Radiation, 83-90
Radiatory, 88
Radioactivity, 82-4, 88, 91
Radium, 83
Rajas, 43, 76
Reaching out, 37
Real, 35, 58
Recognition, 55, 66
Recuperative, 43
Refinement, 7, 35, 75, 88, 91, 117
Relationship, 26, 27, 42, 59, 60, 119, 131
Responsibility, 26, 42, 48, 62, 119
Rest, 7, 16, 42, 43, 76
Restfulness, 43, 75-6, 78, 91
Revelation, 124
Review, 5, 29, 30, 52
Rhythm, 43, 66-7
Right action, 62
Right living, 82
Ring-pass-not, 106
Rose, 14
Rotary motion, 84-8

S

Sacrifice, 97, 120, 123
Sacral center, 20, 81
Samadhi, 67
Sanat-Kumara, 64, 89
Satva, 43
Scheme, planetary, 83
Science, 3, 31, 115, 117
Second ray, 9, 10, 11, 15, 21, 22-4, 26, 42, 55-6, 59, 67, 75, 89, 94, 96, 100-1, 103, 108, 128-132
Seeds, 35
Seed thoughts, 5, 28, 89
Self-aggrandizement, 46
Self-centeredness, 47, 51-2 82, 86, 101
Self-commiseration, 91
Self-conceit, 28, 31, 49, 51-2
Self-concern, 28, 31, 49, 51-2
Self-correction, 105
Self-deception, 58
Self-development, 121
Self-discipline, 56
Self-discovery, 105
Self-effacing, 46, 72
Self-effort, 93
Self-forgetting, 53, 78
Self, Higher, 44
Self-immunization, 29
Self-interest, 31
Selfishness, 45
Self-knowledge, 7
Selfless, 40
Self-preoccupation, 51-2, 61